China on 1

MW00323714

Several thousand years ago Indo–European culture diverged into two ways of thinking; one went West, the other East. Tracing their differences, Christopher Bollas examines how these mentalities are now converging once again, notably in the practice of psychoanalysis.

Creating a freely-associated comparison between Western psychoanalysts and Eastern philosophers, Bollas demonstrates how the Eastern use of poetry evolved as a collective way to house the individual self. On one hand he links this tradition to the psychoanalytic praxes of Winnicott and Khan, which he relates to Daoism in their privileging of solitude and non-verbal forms of communicating. On the other, Bollas examines how Jung, Bion and Rosenfeld assimilate the Confucian ethic that sees the individual and group mind as a collective, while Freudian psychoanalysis, he argues, has provided an unconscious meeting place of both viewpoints.

Bollas's intriguing book will be of interest to psychoanalysts, psychotherapists, Orientalists, and those concerned with cultural studies.

Christopher Bollas is a psychoanalyst and novelist.

China on the Mind

Christopher Bollas

Routledge
Taylor & Francis Group
LONDON AND NEW YORK

First published 2013
by Routledge
27 Church Road, Hove, East Sussex BN3 2FA

Simultaneously published in the USA and Canada
by Routledge
711 Third Avenue, New York, NY 10017

Routledge is an imprint of the Taylor & Francis Group, an informa business

British Library Cataloguing in Publication Data
A catalogue record for this book is available from the British Library

Library of Congress Cataloging in Publication Data
Bollas, Christopher.
China on the mind / by Christopher Bollas.
p. cm.
ISBN 978-0-415-66975-7 (978-0-415-66976-4) 1. Buddhism and
psychoanalysis. 2. China--Civilization. I. Title.
BQ4570.P755B65 2013
150.19'5--dc23
2012017870

ISBN: 978-0-415-66975-7 (hbk)
ISBN: 978-0-415-66976-4 (pbk)
ISBN: 978-0-203-08301-7 (ebk)

Typeset in Times
Typeset by Fakenham Prepress Solutions, Fakenham, Norfolk NR21 8NN

MIX
Paper from
responsible sources
FSC
www.fsc.org   FSC® C004839

Printed and bound in Great Britain by
TJ International Ltd, Padstow, Cornwall

Contents

Acknowledgements

I would like to thank Arne Jemstedt and Camilla Silfverskiöld, from Stockholm, for their support with this project and their assistance in guiding me to Li Yawen of Bejing University who is translating the work into Chinese.

I would like to thank Ken Bruder, a philosopher and long-time friend, for reading the text and commenting on it, and Naohiko Tachi, a Japanese colleague, friend and my translator, for reading the text and providing a critique. Also I am grateful to Tachi and his colleagues in Osaka for their generous reception of myself and my work during my weeks visiting and lecturing in their beautiful city. To Sarah Nettleton, psychoanalyst, for her endless patience reading and commenting on repeated drafts and for her skillfull editing, thank you. The ideas presented in this text, however, are solely the author's and do not necessarily represent the views of those who commented on the book.

To Kate Hawes I am deeply grateful for her encouragement and cooperation during her many years as Senior Editor at Routledge in London and for her immediate and enthusiastic support for this somewhat off-beat book.

I would like to thank the following presses for permission to publish excerpts from their publications:

University of California Press for permission to reproduce material from *The Poems of Mao Zedong*, pp. 65–6 (1997).

Three poems from *The Penguin Book of Japanese Verse* translated by Geoffrey Bownas and Anthony Thwaite (Penguin Books 1964, revised edition 1998, 2009). Translation © Geoffrey Bownas and Anthony Thwaite, 1964, 1998, 2009.

Chinese symbol for war cart from *China: Empire of Living Symbols*, Cecilia Lindquist, Da Capo Press, 1991.

Short extracts of poetry from 'The Festival of Pain' and 'The Abyss of Sound' by Chŏng Hyonjuong and a short extract of poetry from 'The Game and the Moon' by Kim Su-yŏng featured in *Modern Korean Literature*, edited by Peter H. Lee, Honolulu, University of Hawai'i Press, 1990, pp. 46, 161.

'Him I'm Thinking Of', in *Chinese Poetry: An Anthology of Major Modes and Genres*, Wai-Lim Yip, p. 79. Copyright © 1997, Duke University Press. All rights reserved. Reprinted with permission of the publisher. www.dukeupress.edu

Extracts from 'After an Ancient Poem' are taken from *The Selected Poems of Li Po*, translated by David Hinton. Copyright © 1996 by David Hinton. Published by Anvil Press Poetry in 1998.

Extracts from 'The Journey North', 'Adrift', 'Song of the War-Carts', 'The River Village' and 'Two Impromptus' are taken from *The Selected Poems of Tu Fu*, translated by David Hinton. Copyright © 1988 by David Hinton. Published by Anvil Press Poetry in 1990.

'The Yellow Bicycle' (6 lines) from *Praise* by Robert Hass, copyright © 1979 by Robert Hass. Reprinted by permission of HarperCollins Publishers.

Short extracts of poetry by O Cham, Myungok, Ch'On Kŭm, Chu Ŭisik, Pak Hyogwan and Kim Sujang from *The Columbia Anthology of Traditional Korean Poetry*, edited by Peter H. Lee.

Copyright © 2002 Columbia University Press. Reprinted with permission of the publisher.

Short extracts of poetry by Kim Sowol, from *The Columbia Anthology of Modern Korean Poetry*, edited by David R. McCann. Copyright © 2004 Columbia University Press. Reprinted with permission of the publisher.

Short extracts of poetry by Zhuangzi from *Zhuangzi: Basic Writings*, edited by Burton Watson. Copyright © 2003 Columbia University Press. Reprinted with permission of the publisher.

Introduction

This work originated as a series of lectures to be given in Korea in 2010, following a tour of Japan in 2009.

To begin with I thought I would base my talks on readings from key philosophical figures whose works have inspired the Eastern world: Lao Tzu, Confucius, and Zhuangzi in particular, and then consider whether their views had significant links to Western thinking.

However, in the course of preparation for this I began to see a relationship between Eastern thinking and psychoanalytical thought, and the project developed into an attempt to link certain aspects of psychoanalytical practice to Eastern ways of being.

In addition, I became fascinated by the extraordinary emotional and ideational implications of Chinese characters, and my reading of Li Po, Wang Wei, Tu Fu and poets from Korea and Japan introduced me to a form of poetry unique to this part of the world. Not only was I learning about how the East thinks; I was also discovering a way in which it invests mind into poetry, so that by reciting poems people are engaged in a type of open dreaming.

The theme of the work then turned into something of a theory of the mind – the Eastern mind – that seemed to have significant implications for the study of mental processes in the West, and especially for the mental action we term psychoanalysis.

The project was endlessly surprising. As a novice in Eastern studies I found that a new world was opening up for me, but I was also learning things about psychoanalysis that I had never

understood. This book is therefore not only a highly idiosyncratic study of the Eastern way of thinking and living but also
a curious intellectual 'happening' within this author's life as a
psychoanalyst.

Although China has been open to travellers and traders from
the Western world and elsewhere for over four thousand years
it has nonetheless maintained what seems to be a remarkable
isolation. Some of this is credited to the view in ancient
China that it was the centre of the world and superior to all
other cultures, but there are other reasons why China, and
indeed Korea, Japan and other Far Eastern countries, share this
isolation. It is not due to arrogance, nationalism, or insularity. It
is because the people of the Eastern world *think differently* from
the people of the Western world.

This book aims to explore the Eastern mind, but at the outset
we face hazards inherent in dividing the world simplistically into
different ways of thinking, and this author faces that challenge
with trepidation. Is one really justified in using the terms
'Eastern mind', 'Oriental mind', 'Chinese mind' – or, indeed,
'Western mind', 'Occidental mind' or 'European mind'? Such
categories are not only arbitrary and reductionist, they are also –
as this book will, I hope, demonstrate – in certain specific ways
inaccurate. It is an irony of this exploration, then, that I will have
to settle on part-truths in order to develop my argument.

The central idea explored in this book is that when we refer to
a difference between Eastern and Western ways of thinking we
are talking not about different minds but about different *parts*
of the mind. Historically, Eastern thinking has tended towards
forms of thought that are based on 'the maternal order' while
Western thinking reflects forms of thought derived from 'the
paternal order'.

The maternal order refers to the *forms* of knowledge conveyed
to the self as foetus, neonate and infant, prior to the acquisition
of language. This is presentational knowledge. The world, as
thing, presents itself – or is presented – and thus leaves impressions upon the self. The mother, for example, instructs the infant
in countless axioms of being and relating presented through

the logic of her actions. These actions are assimilated by the infant's ego to become formative paradigms that partly govern the infantile self. This knowledge remains resident in all adults and is contiguous to the paternal order.

The various categories of communication experienced by the infant – including sound, vision and physical touch – involve the transformation of affects into emotional experiences that constitute the core of human relations.

The paternal order refers to those categories of communication that are language dependent. These convey the views of the father and, later, the assumptions and laws of society.

Of course, in reality mothers and fathers regularly utilize both of these orders.

Put simply, the Eastern mind favours pre-verbal or non-verbal forms of being, thinking, and relating (the maternal order) while the Western mind generally relies on articulate verbal expression in order to communicate itself and functions in accordance with the paternal order. The Eastern mind uses language to create possible interpretations of meaning and is implicit rather than explicit. The Western mind seeks lucid definitions that are explicit and not meant to be open to the other's readings.

The Eastern mind is founded on five classic books, three of which, *The Book of Songs (or Book of Poems)* (*Shi Jing*), *The Book of Rites (Li Chi)*, *The Book of Changes (I Ching)* become literary structures that embody the Chinese mind. These five 'mother texts', as I will label them, serve as the mental foundation for the writings of Lao Tzu, Confucius, Mo Tzu, Mencius, Zhuangzi and the post-Confucians, whose works have come down to us in the form of collected commentaries by many authors over the centuries. The individual philosophical texts are therefore the work of subcultures, that become known as Daoism, Confucianism, neo-Confucianism and so forth. Given their relation to the mother texts, such long periods of source-based interpretation may be considered 'transitional objects' (to invoke Winnicott) or, more properly, 'transitional moments' with respect to the way the Chinese have developed the body of their rites and their poems to guide them through life.

The Eastern mother texts and their transitional interpreters offer a template for all human beings while the Western mind, although certainly cultivating life forms for traditional purposes, has a fascination with the rogue self, the individual set apart from the group, a challenge to tradition. Eastern discourse is ambiguous, allowing for communication to be co-constructed, whereas Western discourse favours lucidity and a clear distinction between speaker and recipient. The message is thus an indicator of *difference,* an act that separates and demarcates people from one another.

Reflecting on the post-Legalist[1] philosopher, Hsün Tzu[2] (293–235 BCE) who regarded human nature as chaotic and in need of profound ritualization in order to create a guiding social structure, Jacques Gernet concludes 'One can understand the difficulties of the dialogue when the Chinese and European civilizations came into contact with each other in the seventeenth century'.[3]

David Hall and Roger Ames, in their brilliant text *Anticipating China,* maintain that Western thinking is causal and Eastern thinking is correlative. Western logic is metonymic or diachronic; Eastern thought is metaphoric or synchronic. Although in China there were intermittent periods of interest in logic and rational thinking, 'these were soon effectively abandoned in favor of concretely interpersonal exercises in analogical thinking'.[4] The Chinese examined the world in the differing forms of its process, rather than in its substantive differences.

Around 3500 BCE the Indo–European Aryan people entered North India and intermingled with the indigenous population. It was out of this mix that Hinduism arose. C. Scott Littleton[5] argues that they brought with them ideas not dissimilar to those of the Ancient Greeks of that period. It was in the same region, North India, that the Buddha lived in the late 6th and early 5th centuries BCE, and so from this part of the world emerged two great movements: Hinduism and Buddhism.

In approximately 2500 BCE, in Ur in Sumeria (modern Iraq) some 2,000 miles to the west of North India, we discover the first decidedly Western epic: *The Epic of Gilgamesh.* It testifies to the single individual's determination to conquer his world, to make a mark for himself that will last thousands of years. Enkidu runs with the animals and is a man of nature until he is seduced by a woman and forced into civilization. When Gilgamesh defeats Enkidu he therefore conquers the natural world. It will be almost two thousand years before Homer's epics appear, sometime in the 8th century BCE, but there is a clear line of thought from the Sumerian to the Homeric period that concerns the quest-oriented ambitions of the human being. The natural world is to be conquered and man is to make his mark in life through acts of memorable heroism. The emphasis is on the solitary form of the individual self and the tragic realization that even the fullest life is ended by death with no hope for resurrection.

In other words, in this area of the world, with its longstanding communication between many different races and ethnic groups, we can discern one tradition of thought that moves West and one that moves East.

Travelling East in 2000 BCE we enter the spiritual kingdoms of Hinduism and later of Chinese philosophy which emphasize man's obligation to live within the harmony of the natural world and to accommodate and revere it. They understand human life as merely a form of transience.

This is not to say, however, that the Eastern mind has no concept of the individual self; indeed, far from it. Hinduism believes in the *Brahman* or universal soul but also recognizes that this universal principle will exist in each person in a unique way: the inner self or *atman.* It recognizes an interrelation between *dharma* – the ethical, social, and divine order of things, and *kharma* – individual action. In this respect, as I shall argue, Hinduism anticipates and structures the conflict between the individual self and the large group. In China a different set of secular terms will be established in order to negotiate the same conflict.

While the Western epic is based on man's adventures in the external world, testing the strength, stamina, courage and intelligence of the hero, Eastern texts emphasize the ordinary evanescent moments of life's journey. In the Hindu tradition this involves finding the link between one's *atman* and the universal soul of man, and this finding – *moksha* – is regarded as a transcendent act.

Transcendence in the East; heroism in the West.

Both East and West regard human life as a journey, but they differ in their understanding of this. The Western mind explores the material world, discovering new evidence in a never-ending journey that honours its adventurers, who are identified with the found. The emphasis is on a venture that penetrates the real, analyzes and organizes it, and presumes to add to the pool of knowledge. The Eastern mind explores the spiritual world, discovering new internal positions that a self can take in order to instantiate through heightened consciousness ever more inspired forms of the immanental. The aim is to minimize the self's destructive potential, to find through religious forms and ritual actions a route to the generation of a better human being.

In the West, with its tradition of self-representation through words, language is the commerce of intellect. It is democratic; it allows for a shared engagement with the found and it is open to scrutiny. The East's form of self-presentation consists in living itself as an exemplary form. The less said the better, as language indicates a failure to be self-evident through the manner of one's being. In the West to speak is to engage; in the East to speak is to repel.

Throughout this work I shall distinguish between the 'presentational' and the 'representational', between self-presentation and self-representation. Presentation (in any context) is the *form* of a being or a communication; representation refers to the *content* of a communication. The Eastern mind places more emphasis on the presentational and tends to shun the representational, whereas for the Western mind content is the core of communication.

Of course, although East and West diverge in the emphasis they give to many crucial philosophies of life, such distinctions are never absolute. Scholars point out that there are Eastern epics that are built firmly around the accomplishments of the heroic self – the 12th-century Japanese epic *Heike Monogatari* (*Tale of the House of Taira*) has been compared to *The Song of Roland*. Conversely, we can find Western epics that use this idiom for a more spiritual insight into the form of individual life, as do medieval allegories.

The point is not that East and West are utterly dissimilar. In certain ways, Western and Eastern frames of mind still share many qualities in common. Indeed, I shall argue that they developed from a mind that was once unified, and that this original unity offers precedence for the rejoining of the two mentalities. However, the polarities are usefully identified in order for us to see how far the two traditions have emphasized quite different aspects of human being, leading to profound differences in the way the world is viewed.

Both have evolved powerful religions that cultivate orthodox scholars who interpret scripture in prescriptive ways. They share, in other words, a hierarchy within their religions, especially if we compare the arcane schools within the Vedanta school of Hindu philosophy – based on interpretation of the *Upanishads* – with early medieval interpretations of the Bible in the West.

However, although both traditions have their sacred texts, orally transmitted and often set to music, it is significant that in the East it is not only the *content* of the texts that is considered to be holy; the *sound* of them spoken aloud is in itself regarded as a sacred experience. This illustrates again the Eastern emphasis on form.

In the era of Plato and Aristotle, Greek society was centred on the *polis*, where religious edicts had long since been secularized and transformed into objects of debate, and laws were continuously scrutinized in a hotbed of democratic controversy. At the same time China was on the move towards centralization; large populations were glued together by a combination of religion, submission and an ethic that mandated cooperation. The Chinese rarely questioned their laws, and usually shunned any individual's attempts at asserting new ideas that might diminish the power of the authority. Although China did develop its own system of rational thought, one that was notably successful in coordinating new commercial, military and technological realities, it never abandoned the mentality of the archaic period. The ancient and the new continued to walk hand in hand.

Comparing Greece and China between the 5th and 3rd centuries BCE, Jacques Gernet claims that Chinese philosophy may be described as 'organicist'.[6] It is rational but cosmological, absorbed in issues that were of no interest to Western philosophers at the time. Comparing Mencius[7] to the Greeks, Gernet claims that Mencius focused on the complementarity of 'productive and administrative functions'[8] while Greeks were interested in the 'radical opposition' between 'the sensible world and the intelligible' a distinction which the Chinese would 'have rejected ... emphatically as artificial'.[9]

Linguistic impediments, argues Gernet, would have made it difficult for the Chinese to develop a philosophy of being and 'the elaboration of logic'.[10] While the Greeks searched for the Truth, the Chinese followed a different route, concentrating on those elements that ordered the social, natural and cosmic world.

Gernet points out that Greek and Chinese physics attended to very different matters. The Greeks ordered the world in geometric spatial perspectives while the Chinese were more interested in 'the phenomenon of magnetism and vibration, tides, and sonic and seismic waves'.[11] When it came to musical composition the Chinese concentrated on 'the tonal quality of different instruments and ways to construct accurate models of chimes, whereas the Greeks defined the musical scale geometrically.'[12]

Gernet ponders the very question addressed here: does the comparative backwardness of the Chinese in respect, for example, to their lack of interest in logic, represent 'an inferior stage in the evolution of the human mind?'[13] Gernet rejects this assertion but it serves our purpose to point to it. One aspect of the argument proposed in this study is that, although the Western and Eastern minds have evolved very different forms of thought, they are now starting (for many reasons) to turn towards each other, and in so doing can be seen to complement one another, even if such contiguity may be conflicted.

Jean-Pierre Vernant puts it this way: 'It is not that the Chinese did not get so far as the Greeks; they simply advanced in a different direction'.[14] The Greeks valued an ideal man who exemplified the combination of differing attitudes – what Vernant terms the 'agonistic spirit'.[15] The aim to prove oneself above all others, to excel in acts of generosity that become forms of largesse, and above all 'a desire for autonomy and non-servitude'[16] is in stark contrast to the Confucian concept of virtue achieved through the abandonment of human traits – an ideal shared by Zen with its goal of becoming the Buddha.

Vernant cites a fascinating study by André G. Haudricourt[17] that compares East and West based on a fundamental social division: the mentality of herdsmen and sailors versus the mentality of gardeners. The former involves leadership by one figure – men must be led in society as a shepherd guides his flock – while for the gardener the optimal social order reflects a natural order that needs no such intervention.

Hinduism provides, in some senses, a buffer between West and East. Even though it was to have a profound influence on Chinese philosophy, there was from very early on something of Bollywood[18] in its fabulous, soap-like stories of Vishnu and the cast of avatars through whom he appears in drama after drama. The *Ramayana* is perhaps the most famous example of this feature, as the heroic figure of Rama, an incarnation of Vishnu, endures repeated trials of his faith. It is ultimately a religious romance, with Shiva as the perfect anti-hero who will be located in one form after another by the endless inventiveness of the Hindu imagination.

Hinduism is religious surrealism. Set against the respective austerities of Christianity and Buddhism it is refreshingly excessive. There are countless myths of creation, scores of gods and lesser gods, with each small village entertaining its own representations of the deities.

As discussed, in the concepts of *dharma* and *kharma* there is a hint of what is to be passed on to China – and, much later, to Buddhism. *Dharma* refers to the order of the universe and includes religious, social, and ethical action to which men must adhere. *Kharma* is the individual action of man whose spiritual and ethical obligation is to be part of the cosmic order of *dharma*. The Hindu concept of reincarnation – the cycle of birth and rebirth – is not to be found in the West or in the Far East in this form. But it recognizes aims and obligations within a human life, unlike some later Eastern religions, and places value on achieving pleasure and material success in one's human incarnation.

If Hinduism contains aspects of both East and West it is still markedly different from both, containing mental axioms that we may see as a dividing line between East and West. Since this work is to focus on the Far East, I must with regret forego further exploration of Hindu thinking, despite fascinating parallels between its influence in India and the place of Confucianism and Daoism in China.

Zen Buddhism is given less space than it deserves in this text, but it is nonetheless a hugely important bridge in the reconciliation of East and West that is taking place today. Through the concept of *duhka* (the idea that we are transient and that life is suffering), it shares with Christianity an ascetic pessimism about life. However it offers through the concept of *samsara* (rebirth) a connection between human suffering and a realm of pure forms, empty of pain. It is through meditation that one lessens and then transcends *duhka*. When we come to Chinese and Japanese philosophy and poetry, where the suffering of life and its transience are almost unbearably represented, it is easy to see how elements of Buddhism entered China to find a new home after its virtual expulsion from India by Islam.

In Britain in particular, psychoanalysis has focused on the pre-verbal expressions of the analysand, the order of communication that exists between mother and infant. In this way it is closer in its understanding of the self to the Eastern mind than other schools of psychoanalytic thought (for example those of Freud and Lacan) that are more reliant upon the verbal world. I shall develop an argument that the seminal texts of Donald Winnicott and Masud Khan incorporate Eastern forms of thought and being, even though they apparently failed to recognize this antecedent. Whereas Freud privileged self-representation, especially through his emphasis on free association, Winnicott and Khan's praxis was based on self-presentation – on being, or form, as communication. By the end of this book we shall discover, however, the extent to which core axioms of psychoanalysis – even as practised by Freud – can be seen as an unconscious integration of Eastern and Western frames of mind. Psychoanalysis remains largely unaware of this accomplishment.

The text is in three parts.

Part One will consider the Eastern mind from a psychoanalytical perspective by focusing on three of the five mother texts: *The Book of Songs (Shi Jing)*, *The Book of Rites (Li Chi)* and *The Book of Changes (I Ching)*.[19] The other 'classic texts' are *The Book of History (Shu Jing)* and *The Book of Spring and Autumn Annals (Lin Jing)*. A sixth text, *The Book of Music (Yue Jing)* was destroyed during the Warring Period, in the Qin Dynasty (around 231 BCE) when all the classical books were burned. *The Book of Music*, unlike the other texts, could not be recollected.

Part Two will consider the transitional interpreters – Lao Tzu, Confucius, Zhuangzi and others – who both interpret and instantiate the mother texts in their own writings which are then disseminated throughout Chinese culture. These foundational axioms become part of the 'unthought known'[20] of Eastern culture, intrinsic to the collective unconscious mental structures of the Koreans, Japanese and others, even as these countries have developed their own specific traditions and unique histories.

My commentary in Part Two will depart from the more customary critical review with a more associative process as I link these writings to contemporary psychoanalytical thinking.

Part Three will then examine the social psychology of the individual and the group mind and consider ways in which the burgeoning interest in psychoanalysis in China and the Far East is a more natural intellectual evolution than one might imagine.

This book is therefore a blend of traditional Eastern writings, Western psychoanalytical texts, and my own idiomatic readings of both. Weaving their way through this work will be strands of divergence, previewed above, as well as converging threads. One of the divergent strands will concern the particular function of poetry in the Eastern world and its place as representative of the Eastern mind. One of the convergent strands will be the emergence of prose fiction – first in China and then in the West – that differs from poetic structures even as it begins in verse form.

I shall emphasize that poetry is fundamentally presentational (form takes precedence over content) while narrative fiction is representational (content takes precedence over form). These two forms, the poetic and the fictive narrative, will be linked to two very different elements within the practice of psychoanalysis, something that in itself can be seen to bridge East and West.

Poetry provides the background to my argument that the psychoanalytical process has its own poetics of form that links to Eastern ways of being. However, I also believe that one cannot begin to understand the Eastern mind without a close study of the nature and function of poetry in their societies. 'Poetry in China is the Great Wall' writes Willis Barnstone.[21] 'It holds in Chinese civilization' he continues, a point that I shall develop from a psychoanalytical perspective.

Although *The Book of Songs* is less a collection of poetry and more an album of popular ballads, it is the beginning of a poetic tradition in China that ramifies throughout the Far East. Ballads and song will give way to more complex poetic structures – such as *Yueh-fu* which begins in the Han Dynasty and lasts for 700 years or more. Although they will, from time to time, be subjected to musical imposition, where lines must follow a musical logic rather than a poetic thought line, during the great period of Chinese writing (the 8th century CE) poets such as Li Po, Wang Wei, Tu Fu create poems that were always *there* in the Chinese process of thought. I hope to illuminate why that was so.

The reader will note that I may introduce on the same page poets from different eras and from different countries. This may seem oddly higgledy piggledy, but by juxtaposing poems in this way I believe that it is possible to demonstrate something timeless and shared between peoples who are separated by centuries and national boundaries. This text will be punctuated by poetry, disrupted by it if you will; a descriptive reference is a poor substitute for the reality of a poem.

Finally, why have I chosen China for my title, given that Korea, Japan, Vietnam and other Eastern countries have their own unique traditions?

In China there are hundreds of dialects and, until very recently, the inhabitants of the different regions could not necessarily understand each other's spoken tongue. However, for thousands of years they all used the same written script which brought them together. As Jacques Gernet points out, written Chinese was also the official language of Vietnam until the French invasion, and of Korea until the Japanese invasion, and it was used by the Japanese during their occupation of China. Educated Japanese read Chinese. 'Its cursive forms' writes Gernet 'served as the foundation of the Japanese syllabaries and the Korean alphabet'.[22]

From the 14th through to the early 20th century civil servants in China had to sit an exam on Confucius's *Analects*. Until the early 20th century students in Korea, Japan, and Vietnam also had to sit national exams on the *Analects*. Simon Leys claims that 'no book in the entire history of the world has exerted, over a longer period of time, a greater influence on a larger number of people than this slim little volume'.[23]

Even as one respects the very real differences between the countries of the East, it is clear, therefore, that China has inevitably been *on* or *in* the minds of the people of the Far East. This text will explore ways in which they have been influenced psychologically by Chinese thought as well as considering what the Western psychotherapeutic world may have to learn from this profound intellectual dissemination.

Modern China is very much on the mind of the so-called globalized community as it anticipates the impact of Chinese industry and its meteoric economic growth. But along with these new developments the Chinese will bring with them – at the very least in their collective unconscious – those mother texts and ethical axioms that have formed the fabric of their life for thousands of years. What could their particular unthought known bring to the long-held views within the West?

In the brief period of 100 years during which psychoanalysis has become the core introspective philosophy of the West, how do we understand its intriguing *unconscious* integration of Eastern and Western frames of mind?

The maternal order that is foundational to psychoanalysis has been subjected to an ongoing repression within the psychoanalytical movement, but since this presents an Eastern way of being and relating, is it possible that growing commerce between West and East will de-repress the maternal order and challenge the hermeneutically-bound, causal-inclined paternal focus that has so dominated psychoanalytic discourse?

These are the questions that guide this work. It needs to be said, however, that I am not a Sinologist and although I have taken considerable care to be certain of the research I have read, anyone studying China or Oriental thought is presented with a thicket of problems. There are, for example, multiple spellings for the same surname. I have sometimes assumed that I was reading a philosopher I had not encountered before, only to discover that it was in fact the work of one I had already read, but the name, translation, and format were so completely different as to be unrecognizable. Add to this a contest over just how many foundational texts are 'classics' (is it four, five or six?) and the widely different names assigned to them, and we see why anyone who attempts a scholarly text on China or Eastern thought should feel daunted.

I do not address here the long history in the West of people involved in psychoanalysis, gestalt psychology and the psychotherapies who have studied Eastern thought. There is a significant psychoanalytical literature on Buddhist thought, including the writings of Carl Jung, Erich Fromm, Karen Horney, Harold Kelman, Nina Coltart and Mike Eigen. Some of their essays have been assembled by Anthony Molino in *The Couch and the Tree* (New York: North Point Press, 1998). There are many fine works by American Buddhists that link psychoanalysis and Zen, especially Jeffrey Rubin, *Psychotherapy and Buddhism* (New York: Plenum Press, 1996); Mark Epstein, *Thoughts Without a Thinker* (New York: Basic Books, 1995); and more recently Joseph Bobrow, *Zen and Psychotherapy: Partners in Liberation* (New York: W.W. Norton, 2010) and Pilar Jennings, *Mixing*

Minds: The Power of Relationships in Psychoanalysis and Buddhism (Boston: Wisdom Publications, 2010). These works are part of a long project, as it were, of Western practitioners connecting threads to Eastern thought, especially to Zen. That tradition focuses on highly specific ways in which Zen and forms of meditation connect to psychoanalysis and extend it.

For every book written on the topic there are scores of clinical study groups and centres that meditate and think about these issues. And for every group there are scores of individuals who think about these issues in solitude and build into their practice those aspects supplied by one's unconscious singularity.

My work is therefore not intended to be inclusive. It is thesis driven; an essay.

Part One

Preconceptions

Chapter 1

Moments

'The Chinese mind, as I see it at work in the *I Ching*', writes
Jung, 'seems to be exclusively preoccupied with the chance
aspects of events.'[1] In his analysis of the differences between the
Chinese and Western minds, Jung finds the Chinese to be interested less in causal logic than in the overdeterminations of life:
'The moment under actual observation appears to the ancient
Chinese view more of a chance hit than a clearly defined result
of concurrent causal chains'. According to Jung, the Chinese
concept of the moment necessitates portrayal of the 'minutest
nonsensical detail, because all of the ingredients make up the
observed moment.'

The *I Ching* is not the work of a single person but the effort of
a civilization to conceive its view of mankind. China sustained
this collective thinking through the figure of Confucius, whose
Analects become the work of hundreds of commentators over
thousands of years.

Legend has it that the *I Ching* began with Fu Xi who ruled
in about 2500 BCE. It was then reworked by Yu (2194–2149
BCE), who added 52 hexagrams to Fu Xi's original eight.[2] The
text lives in the realm of a game. Each throw of the stalks gives
chance a meaning. There are eight horizontal columns, each
with a different trigram figure and eleven vertical columns: the
trigram figure, the binary value, the name, translations, image
in nature, family relationship, body part, attribute, state and
animal. The first three lines of the hexagram are viewed as the

inner aspect of change while the last three lines are viewed as the outer aspect of change. The change that is described through the actions of the *I Ching* plays the inner or personal aspect of the human being against the group situation.

Sixty four hexagrams constitute the modern *I Ching,* each accompanied by a commentary articulated over the ages. Each represents a distinct aspect of lived experience: the creative, the receptive, difficulty at the beginning, youthful folly, waiting, conflict, the army, holding together, small taming, treading[3] – to name the first ten.

We journey through these experiences that characterize life. Inner states of mind and outer features of the world converge because such moments move us then leave us. 'We the living, we're passing travellers' writes Li Po (701–762 CE) in 'After an Ancient Poem'.[4] He is expressing the view of the self-as-traveller that had existed at least for a thousand years before him and would still be recognized as a theme in China today.

The *I Ching* is the universe in miniature, governed by three principles: Simplicity, Variability and Persistency. The world we live in, and by which we are changed, is very simple: it is always moving and yet it is invariant.

As mentioned in the introduction, the *I Ching* is one of five surviving ancient foundational texts that constitute the background of the Chinese literary tradition and distil the fundamental axioms of Chinese thought. These serve as the points of embarkation for the origin, evolution, and structuralization of the Chinese mind.

To explain what I mean, let us return in more detail to the *I Ching*.

The reeds (later lines) of the *I Ching* were either straight or broken. To embody an image or an idea reeds would vary in the composition of these lines in what to a Western eye would be three-line stanzas: a trigram.

Eventually two trigrams would be combined into hexagrams.

As Hellmut and Richard Wilhelm illustrate in their seminal work *Understanding the I Ching,*[5] the first trigram, called Ch'en – eldest son – looks like this:

— —
— —
———

However, as with all trigrams it stands for a lot more than the literal eldest son. It also signifies 'evoking', thunder and the wish of the female element (Kun) to be impregnated and to give birth to a son. It has a colour: dark yellow. It is also associated with ideas of power, speed and being outstanding, and with images such as a white horse, a person's foot, the spring, and a road that leads to some intended point.

We can see how this one trigram is a cluster of ideas or associations. At no time when it is constituted (out of stalks) or written down could it ever possibly mean just one thing. What it means will be determined partly by the context in which it is composed and partly by the way anyone interprets it. From a psychoanalytical perspective a trigram is an 'overdetermined' presentation that has condensed many diverse ideas into a single image. *Why* they belong together is purely a matter of an individual self's encounter with the chances delivered to him or her within the real.

A trigram is a form of thought or – thought as form. Within the realm of these images that overlay one another, a person utilizing it will be *thinking* his or her own unique thoughts through the trigram's intrinsically poetic structure. It bears striking resemblance to Freud's theory of unconscious contents as a mental organization composed of 'clusters of ideas'. Chance, or change, is built into this system of symbolization as its meaning is open both to the moment in which it is constituted and to the mental idiom of the interpreter.

When trigrams were put together to form hexagrams the meaning became even more radically changeable. 'A combination of trigrams determines the image belonging to the hexagram in question' write the Wilhelms, 'the image being made up of the meanings and inner dynamisms of the two trigrams'.[6]

Although a hexagram would seem to be composed of two separate sets of clusters (two trigrams), in fact lines 2, 3 and 4 would constitute a separate, new trigram, as would lines 3, 4 and 5. This system of meaning is a cluster of ideas and images that is always changing as it is combined into hexagrams.

The dynamism of the trigrams is further determined by the intrinsic meaning of a broken or a straight line. A straight line means 'yes', a broken line means 'no.' A straight line means 'creative', a broken line means 'receptive.' And so it goes, with each aspect carrying with it a dynamic associative set in a binary system that partly organizes the clusters of images and ideas.

If the trigram is one form for thinking about lived experience, the hexagram becomes far too complex for conscious thinking alone. It will inevitably be open to unconscious lines of thought; indeed, the hexagram *objectifies unconscious thought*. It is a part of the mental function of the self so that anyone turning to the hexagram is contacting a culturally founded part of the human mind. This is rather like considering a dream: another mental event derived from the chance events of a single day.

It would be quite easy for our interests in the *I Ching* to take up the remainder of this text. We will limit ourselves, however, to musing on its psychic meaning. It is a work that identifies the *foundations* and *qualities* of lived experience, identifying the actual (such as the earth, air, fire, water, fields, etc.) as well as the emotional (such as yearning, longing, fleeing). It is, in effect, a representation of the world, and the game – of throwing the stalks to see what meaning might derive – mirrors the aleatory nature of human life, composed of a series of disconnected chance moments.

For Jung, the hexagram 'was the exponent of the moment in which it was cast ... an indicator of the essential situation prevailing at the moment of its origin.' This feature of the *I Ching* reminds him of his theory of 'synchronicity'. This is Jung's 'concept that formulates a point of view diametrically opposed to that of causality [in that it] ... takes the coincidence of events in space and time as meaning something more than mere chance, namely, a peculiar interdependence of objective events among themselves as well as the subjective (psychic) states of the observer or observers.'[7]

Jung's insights are thought-provoking. Western and Eastern minds would appear to represent opposite traditions of thought, to be incompatible. Eastern thinking is invested in the liminal power of the single moment, in the temporality of transience. The Western mind is founded on linear continuity; temporality is seen as the passage of time necessary for accomplishments. Just as the spiritual potential of life in the moment seems lost to the Western mind, the Eastern mind would appear to have little interest in the sequential logic of Western discourse.

If the human mind has split into two dominant traditions (Western and Eastern), each performing vital functions specific to their tasks but ultimately capable of complementarities, then the Eastern mind is invested in thinking about life in one way while the Western mind thinks of it differently.

One of the ironies of the Chinese mental evolution is that emphasis on the moment rather than upon duration evolved over a thousand years of major upheaval, from the Age of the Warring States (5th century to 3rd century BCE)[8] through the Han Empire and beyond, as hundreds of thousands of Chinese were relocated to the North and elsewhere, either to defend the country against the Mongols or to redistribute the population.[9] However, throughout these disruptions the mother texts were referred to and updated as philosophers, including those whose writing appeared in the name of Confucius, Lao Tzu, or Zhuangzi and poets such as Li Po, Wang Wei and Tu Fu, used them as axioms of thought.

Few poets evoke the naked helplessness of the self in the face of traumatic social disruption (war, dislocation, poverty) as well as the great Chinese poet Tu Fu (712–770 CE).

'The Journey North' begins: 'Heaven and earth are racked with ruin, / sorrow and sorrow, no end in sight'.[10] Tu Fu's poems congeal the extreme mental pain of lives determined by forces of dislocation resulting in long periods of time away from one's family. In 'Adrift' he writes: 'Each departure like any other, where is / my life going in these isolate outlands?'[11] In his harrowing poem 'Song of the War Carts' he conjures the imagery of war that defines lives: 'War carts clatter and creak, / horses stomp and splutter – / each wearing quiver and bow, the war-bound men pass.'[12] Set against the unrelenting grimness of daily life, Tu Fu takes solace in single moments arriving from a different frame of mind. He alludes to this in 'The Journey North' referring to 'my Peach Blossom nostalgia',[13] or in 'The River Village' when he writes 'On long summer days, the business of solitude / fills this river village',[14] or in 'Two Impromptus' when he speaks from deep within all of us: 'in idleness, I become real'.[15]

Tu Fu, like other poets and philosophers, is tenacious in his determination to hold on to the integrity of the single blissful moment of being at one with nature and within oneself. Without such moments the din of mass movements, of social upheavals and the daily grind of poverty threatens to eradicate spiritual being.

One of the distinctive characteristics of Oriental poetry is this concentration on vivid transient experiences: an autumn leaf falling from a tree, a white egret standing still in the water, a cloud passing in the sky. If man is the corrupt force destroying the natural world, such not-man objects allow people to find and to project their need for love and care into the landscape. A stream, a bird, a leaf are not simply objects; they are storehouses for the self's soul.

Twenty-two centuries after Tu Fu's work, in the ironic and moving text of Lu Xun's[16] *The True Story of Ah Q*, we find the Chinese still absorbed in the pathos of human transience. Ah Q, the absurdist protagonist of Lu Xun's work, lives a life of serial chances governed apparently by the mind of a simpleton – until his tragic death awakens the reader to the fact that Ah Q is everyman. We are all simpletons, enduring the pathos of our beginning, our middle and our end.

From a psychoanalytical perspective, to play the *I Ching* is to enact the transient nature of our common lives. Yet, it allows us to feel that we are part of a structure that preceded us, will endure after our death, and of which we have been a constituent. Put differently, it is the Chinese way of thinking about the liminal feature of human experience.

We will become, as Li Po puts it in 'After an Ancient Poem',[17] 'bleached bones' that 'lie silent', but both before and after we lament the limits of our time on earth, 'this life's / phantom treasure shines beyond knowing'.

In what way?

Each of us is chance personified.

Each a 'one-off', amidst the vast population of lived others who have preceded us and will go on in the stream of life. The *I Ching* allows us to play the game of life. We cast the coins and play the *I Ching* just as we go to Vegas to try our luck.

Part of the game is the reading of chance. What is the balance of Yin and Yang in the thrown?

To a psychoanalyst, the game allows the self the illusion of mastering what cannot be controlled. By converting life into a game we live to play another day. The reality, that one day we shall no longer be around to throw the *I Ching*, is subordinated to a game that celebrates chance and insists it is always meaningful. So, maybe death does not triumph after all? If we embrace the aleatory and discern its meaning, the finality of death can be mitigated by an endless chain of significance, by an armada of moments that have cast us in the sands of time. We may not as individuals be recalled for who we are, but our hexametric being is inscribed in the universe.

It is not simply a metaphor for the diverse idioms of a human life; playing this game is to unfold in the fields of variant human experience. The coin thrower goes through 'the changes' and, as his moment is interpreted, he experiences both his own initial reaction to his hexagramatic destiny and its fateful meaning. Throwing and throwing and throwing again, we discover how destiny is intertwined with fate. However much we follow the logic of our idiom (our destiny driven by the urge to elaborate our innate pattern),[18] chance intervenes and the course of life is inevitably changed. Each throwing is an action-thought that enables us to think our existence.

If fate is the moment when destiny meets chance and is redirected, then the *I Ching* stages this everyday experience. The Oriental mind recognizes this simple fact of life. The *ur*-text of the West – the story of Oedipus – finds no simplicity in chance. Indeed, Western literature proposes an endless struggle between the idiom of the self, with its drive to be fulfilled through lived experience, and the fate that will always thwart it. To the Western eye chance is an invitation to tragic outcome. In the East it is a simple feature of life that joins the participants – human and otherwise – in a passing moment.

Unlike the work of Lao Tzu or Confucius, the *I Ching* barely survived into modern times with its reputation intact. Reviled by neo-Confucians and Daoists it was revived through Buddhism in China, Korea, and Japan. Even so, it is not as revered as the works of the Daoists, Confucians, or Zen Buddhists. This may be because it is offered in the form of a game, seeming to play lightly with the human dimension.

Chapter 2

Self as Poem

The Book of Songs (*Shi Jing*) begins with praise for the kings and the elite of China, but the latter two thirds of the work celebrate the travails, tribulations and accomplishments of ordinary man. Assembled over centuries, the book was for the most part compiled by the ruling monarch who would send scribes to the villages to record the songs, hymns and poems of the working people. In this way, the soul of a people was integrated into one document that became a foundational text for China and set a thought form for the Eastern mind. It provided an understanding of the role of poetry in the self's relation to the group, and of the sanctity of the poem as a home for the self – a self that otherwise appeared regulated as part of a collective will. As David Hinton writes 'it is a secular poetry having a direct personal voice speaking of immediate and concrete experience, and it is a poetry that functions as a window onto the inner life of a person.'[1]

The *Book of Songs* dates from around 1000 BCE. In its early days, before it was burned during the Qin dynasty, it may have included as many as 3,000 songs. Confucius edited the edition we have today which consists of 305 poems and songs, and minor editing in his name took place over a further 600-year period. It is unique; a melodic record of the basics of human life such as love, sacrifice, work, marriage and combat.

Hall and Ames point out that when reading any of the major philosophical texts people would break into song and dance. Songs would 'invest... claims with passion'[2] and glue the population into a group formed around an intense sonic resonance embedded in poems.

Intriguingly, although these poems became canonical and were shared by everyone they are nonetheless governed by the inherent ambiguity of Chinese characters. Each person would read the poem in a highly individual manner, private self and social self intermingling through the unique effect of Chinese linguistic expression.

Poems conveyed hidden meanings during periods of political turmoil. When there was conflict between kings or feuding lords, when 'leaders wished to express or validate their own positions, they would sometimes couch the message within a poem',[3] a tradition that passed to Korea and Japan.

The three ancient poetic traditions in Korea – *hyangga, koryo* and *sijo* – were spoken or sung by the people. By dealing with issues that were common to everyone – love, loss, evanescence, death – songs brought people together, eventually providing highly structured forms that were ingrained in the minds of those who sang and listened to them.

By singing, the individual joins the group as an embodied presence. We sing with our bodies. (The stanza structures of *The Book of Songs* were constructed to fit with musical form and with dance steps.) Such passion imbues the philosophy of the East as ideas are transmitted through a collective sense of the ordinary shared details of lived experience. Body, self, family, village and mass society *think* through poetic structure, an act that integrates private and social experience.

For Confucius the correct path is a matter of how one lives rather than what one achieves. This precedence of form over content is transmitted generationally, not through the subject of the poetry but through the aesthetics of poetic structure, which can be seen as a silent means of guiding a self through The Way (The Dao).[4]

Do these songs embody a 'thought pattern' (to quote Jung) or a template for the mind? Could it be the aim of the Oriental mind to evolve mental structures rather than to communicate discursive discourse, as in the Occidental tradition?

Sharp distinctions may be hazardous, but there seems to be a radical difference between the aim of such songs (and of other Oriental forms, such as *haiku*) and the exemplary message conveyed by the Western epic poem. The epic tells of man's quest for meaning. A hero – Odysseus, Aeneas, Gawain – sets out on a journey, is tested and, almost as an aside, reveals something about living a life. The meaning resides in the content – in the message conveyed by the story. The Oriental tradition, comparatively bereft of such tales, seems devoted to the creation of musical word-structures that take the self through intense experiences that involve the whole being.

If Confucius and others were developing the Oriental mind, then their sayings, songs and poetry are all exercises of that mind. The aim is not to tell a story but to be inhabited by the mentality of the telling: to experience this particular form. In this way self and other, individual and group, region and nation, one country and another, develop and share the same mental processes even though they will differ in their histories.

The poem especially is a vital part of mental life. To hear a poem is to think unthought known experiences; as essential to a Chinese person as language itself. Most of our thoughts are unthinkable in consciousness without language. The Chinese could not think the experiences of their life without the idiom of the poem.

This assumption is based on the idea of the presence of the mother-thought in life. Such structures sustain the type of communication that derives from the mother's way of being with her infant. In the Korean poem 'Maternal Love' by O Cham (1274–1308), the poet compares the father and the mother and writes that 'in love the mother surely surpasses.'[5] O Cham does not mean that the mother is a better person than the father, but that the realm of the maternal surpasses that of the paternal, just as form surpasses content.

My favourite form of ancient Korean poetry is *sijo*, prevalent from the 15th century onwards. After the 18th century it came to be composed of four metric units, with a slight caesura at the end of the second line and an emphatic one at the end of the fourth.

There is also a powerful and vivid 'syntactical division ... in the third line in the form of a counter-theme, paradox, resolution, judgment, command or exclamation.'[6]

The subject matter usually marks a transitional dimension in the natural world – a moment in love life or an expression of sorrow or loss. The *sijo* poet Myungok[7] in the late sixteenth century begins an unnamed poem thus: 'They say dream visits / are 'only a dream' but the longing to see her love is killing her, so 'where else do I see him but in dreams?' and so please come to me in my dreams again and again. The poem's second stanza dwells on the snow falling on a mountain village, burying the path. Why open the gate? No one will be coming. Only my friend, 'a slice of bright moon'.[8]

Another poem by Ch'On Kŭm begins: 'Night draws near in a mountain village / a dog barks far away'.[9] It takes two separate realities of the moment – dusk and a dog barking – and combines them to create an emotional sensation only possible if these two respective contents are brought together in the form of this poem.

A distinctive feature of *sijo* is the way the poets play upon our dream life.

'If the path of my dreams / left footprints'[10] writes Yi Myŏnghan (1596–1645) the road outside the house would be worn down.

'What is life, I ponder' writes Chu Ŭisik (1675–1720), 'it is just a dream!' All good things and bad, are 'dreams within a dream.' But if this is so, well ... 'why not enjoy this dreaming?[11]

'If my lovesick dream' writes Pak Hyogwan (1850–1880) were to be embodied in a cricket on an autumn night it would wake the poet's love in the night. The lover pines – 'the sound sleep that has forgotten me' – as he is excluded from his beloved's dreams. Then, 'she came to my dream' but when he awoke she was gone. Where is she? Who knows? 'Dreams may be empty, / but visit me as often as you can'.[12]

Sijo poems were sung and passed down the generations. Like all oral poetry they varied from place to place and through time. As such, they were somewhere between a private or social dreaming and an object to be perceived as a thing-in-itself, out there in the real. Life is a dream, dreams are dreams within the dream of life. Like poems, dreams come from our imagination. *Sijo* poems come to the Koreans through the song of their mothers and fathers, in early childhood and throughout life. They pass them on to their children; the poems constitute the stream of human existence.

When we are alone we can sing our poems and console ourselves. Perhaps we are never alone. Kim Sujang, who lived in the late 17th century, captures the Eastern sense of solitude:

> In my quiet grass hut,
>   I sit alone.
> The clouds are dozing
>   to the low melody of my song.
> Who else is there that can know
>   the subtle intent of my life?[13]

Throughout the poetic traditions of the East, there is a haunting thread of the liminal aspects of human experience, the space between moments of being, and the ultimate reality that we too are only in between the dead and the unborn. This theme *is* Eastern consciousness, transmitted from fathers to family members, from one person to another, from village head to villagers, from a monarch to his people. The East as a group has developed a shared ability to integrate the visceral realities of the everyday, to hew them into deep philosophical wisdom, and to connect self and large group through the shared reality of human mortality.

In Eastern culture the poem houses a self's individual being. To illustrate how a self comes to live in the poem, or how a poem becomes the self, we shall read a few Eastern poems that, to my mind, help convey this argument.

And although, in comparison to the West, the Eastern individual voice can seem tenuous as a thing in itself, some of the most deeply moving and singular voices are to be found within the otherwise formal harmonic order imposed by Eastern literary forms. I have mentioned the agonizing poetry of Tu Fu. A Japanese equivalent would be the work of Yamanoue Okura who lived in the so-called 'primitive period' before the 8th century. His poem 'Pining for his son Furuhi' is one of the greatest poems I can think of in any literature at expressing the self's love for a child and the unbearable pain of watching the child die a slow and agonizing death. Okura writes:

> I stood, I jumped, I stamped,
> I shrieked, lay on the ground,
> I beat my breast and wailed.
> Yet the child I held so tight
> Has flown beyond my clasp.
> Is this our world's way?[14]

No doubt this poem was disseminated throughout Japan and, as with most Eastern poems, it would have become known by large numbers of the population. Poetry has played more precise a role in Japanese life than in any other culture in the world. Almost all the Emperors wrote poems, the head of the family was obliged to write poems, people communicated by writing them to one another. This tradition continued for many generations until the development of prose in the 20th century.

Perhaps inspired by *The Book of Songs,* the Japanese collected poems from ordinary life and bound them into huge volumes that were disseminated across the country. In 905 CE, the *Kokinshu* (*Poems Ancient and Modern*) contained 1,111 short individual verses. They follow the *tanka* form (an ancient precursor to *haiku*) and they are divided into volumes organized around different themes: the seasons, nature and love.[15] The mentality of an entire era is inscribed in this work.

Sometimes poems were written by groups of people, such as *Poems by Frontier Guards and Their Families* (Nara period) in which individuals – 'a guard' or 'the wife of a guard' – put into four or six lines their personal grief over their fate. 'Oh that I'd had / A moment to paint / A picture of my wife' writes Mononobe Furumaro.[16]

Yet as we witness these remarkable *collections* of poetry that reflect *collective thinking* and become part of the intellect of the *collective* society we also note an interesting transformation. The poems are at times almost too intense and too painful to read. Increasingly, through the *tanka* form and then *haiku*, the poet conceals the self inside the poem.

In the Hein Period (794–1185 CE), the poet Ariwara Yukihira[17] writes:

I must depart now.
But, like the pine
At the peak of Inaba,
Should I hear you pine for me
I shall return to you.

The Japanese word for pine is 'matsu' and refers both to the pine tree and to pining thus playing on a double meaning. We see here a projection of an individual feeling into an object that contains the feeling.

The displaced guard wishes he could paint a picture of his wife. Tourists often joke at the Japanese, toting cameras around the world to take endless snapshots of objects. But these brief poems are themselves dense emotional pictures of personal life projected into common elements of the natural world: a pine tree, an egret, a stream, a fish.

While the Eastern mind sustains a mistrust in wordy communication it invests immense energy in word-pictures that receive a self. This remarkable collective act celebrates the pain, suffering, joy, and transience of every person's life through a communal juxtaposition of common objects. And each poet finds a unique *way* or *form* in which to create his pictures. In this respect, the East has found a way of developing the collective mind while preserving individual idiom. And although the poet may be Japanese or Korean, these poems inherit and develop the unique psychological reality of the Chinese character.

Preoccupied over millennia with transience, the Eastern mind has invested the poem with the poignancy of the evanescent.

Haiku leaves a deep pictorial-emotional impression upon the self. It is gone but it reverberates and becomes timeless. Like the process of mourning, it intensifies a *picturing* of the lost. It is as if the unconscious offers us an inner *haiku* of the person who has left us, as if poetry is so close to the unconscious and to unconscious knowledge that, if we take part in it, as writers or as listeners, we are guided by its wisdom.

Traditionally in the East, any desire to make an individual name for oneself is seen as evidence of shameful egotism. In Zen Buddhism the individual is meant to give up the ego, to dissolve into Buddha. Were people *only* to do this then the self would be eliminated through a process of abstraction. But through a remarkable act of unconscious intelligence the person's being is transformed instead, through poetry, into its representatives in the natural world; individual idiom is transferred into selected poetic objects. That idiom can be detected in the poetry throughout the ages, not in the specific objects themselves but in the form through which the poet arranges them, each act conjuring from pared-down language an intense emotional experience.

In this way, generations have worked to create a mentality that will both house the individual and weave him into the world within which he lives and from which he must depart. It is a stunning accomplishment.

Poetry *presents* the self. It is a way of presenting one's being without having to speak it directly.

The great Korean poet Kim Su-yŏng, who died in 1968, captures the battle between the self of the non-verbal realm and the self that would be verbal. It is as if in his poetry we find a collision between the presentational and the representational orders. In 'The Game and the Moon'[18] an old man watches a child spinning a top and mourns the moment when it stops. He wishes it could go on and on. The child is 'sunk in thought', oblivious to the world around him, while the man is 'mindful of the weight my age accords.' 'A top spins', he writes, 'And makes me cry.' He feels so far removed from the world of the child and says, 'I need some revision of my fate, my mission.' Kim Su-yŏng struggles to find words for wordless emotional truths.

This poem-speech, a language more familiar in the East than the West, privileges the self's being (form) rather that its verbal expression (content).

Poetry shares with psychoanalysis the intersection of the presentational and the representational orders. Most poems share well-known themes; they are re-presentations of existing ideas. But the form of any communication is presentational. It does not re-present anything; it has not existed before. Similarly, people in analysis will share many typical themes – hence the ability of Freud and others to construct theses about the common mental issues of mankind – but no two analysands, or two poets, present these themes in the same way.

Consideration of some aspects of the Chinese language may help us to understand how a character presents its reality, and to appreciate the crucial position of poetry as the core expression of self.

In the West we learn an alphabet of 26 letters. One of the first songs American children learn in school is 'ABCD-EFG-HIJK-LMNOP …' Singing the letters gives them phonetic identity. The sounds of the letters are linked sonically to one another, and this helps connect the appearance of the unfamiliar written script with a familiar sound. Children know how to speak and now they are learning how to write: the dead characters on the blackboard are enlivened by singing.

The Chinese child has to learn 3,000 ideograms.

Each ideogram was originally (and to some extent is still) a picture of a thing, but over time it has acquired many other associations and has become open to multiple meanings. Each is also a unique emotional experience that sets in motion a constellation of related ideas, feelings and historic significances. The characters are rather like the trigrams and hexagrams of the *I Ching*. A character is a thought-world open to ramifying idiosyncratic meaning as it is employed in any moment.

Western children learn to write by transforming letters into words, and Chinese children do *something* of the same, but there is a crucial difference. The Chinese characters are forms of painting and the children learn to use ink and brushes with great skill as they draw the characters. Some ideograms are made up of over twenty strokes. Bearing in mind that each character is ideographic and emotional, the mere act of learning to write is akin to a psychic identification, usually unconscious, with the entire history of that fragment of a nation's emotional life.

I learned this by studying just one character. Having read the haunting and deeply moving poems of Tu Fu, I was struck in particular with his image of the din of war carts thundering through his village. When I saw the image for the war cart in Cecilia Lindquist's beautiful book[19] on Chinese symbols, I studied it for a very long time.

rumble, roar

The ideogram means 'rumble, roar' and I think one can see it as an image of three carts bunched up together. Lindquist focuses on 'how tiresome the noise of carts must have been for the inhabitants of large trading towns, as well as for those making long journeys across the plains'[20] but for Tu Fu they are the icons of war and they convey the feeling of terror.

As the brilliant scholar Wai-Lim Yip[21] points out, the Chinese language is tenseless, it has a minimal syntactical structure, there are no pronouns and no prepositions. In poetry, the Chinese mind intends not to make a point, but instead to create a previously non-existent reality. By reading Yip's presentations of Chinese poems one can gain a deeper understanding of the different way the Chinese people think. To give just one example, he takes a single line from a poem by Wang Wei. Character by character it reads as follows:

Empty   mountain   not   see   man

He then illustrates how one typical translator translates Wang Wei:

There seems to be no one on the empty mountain.

Yip's point is that the Wang Wei lines are never *intended* to be linked into a single syntactical structure. The free-standing nature of each image, the surprising juxtaposition of objects, is a thing unto itself that has an evocative integrity.

The poetic line above could mean many things. And each reader will have his or her own deeply personal experience of it.

Each word enacts its meaning. Empty is *empty*, but then it is next to 'mountain' which seems so full. 'Not' enacts any 'no' at this moment that might link 'empty' with 'mountain' and 'see' 'man' is an enigmatic presentation, with no link to the other images. Taken together, however, they form a previously non-existent cluster of images that hold the reader in the spell of this uncanny verbal act.

Yip stresses that poems are more like sculptures, or montages, or 'mobile points of view in the perceiving act.' He continues, 'The Chinese poets give paramount importance to the acting-out of visual objects and events, letting them explain themselves by their coexisting, coextensive emergence from nature'.[22]

These poems inherit and use the ideographic nature of the Chinese language; each character is itself a small poem. They unite image and sound with personal emotion and yet weave the particular into the social order. A brief poem can thus be both unique and universal at the same time; the perfect gift, whether to a loved one or to a stranger.

This way of thinking through poetic form has had a wide influence in contemporary western poetry. Let me quote from one stanza of Robert Hass's poem 'The Yellow Bicycle'[23] which would not have been possible, in my view, had Hass not been deeply influenced by Eastern poetics:

Sun, sunflower,
coltsfoot on the roadside,
a goldfinch, the sign
that says Yield, her hair,
cat's eyes, his hunger
and a yellow bicycle.

Each line presents a free-standing image. The six lines taken as a whole create a cluster of disparate objects – sunflower, coltsfoot, goldfinch, Yield sign, and so forth – that become a thought. We do not know *what* is thought but we are taken up in the thinking of it, drawn into the matrix of unconscious affinities that have met with experiences in the real.

The poem is the Eastern mentality embodied; each person a poem, the sound of voice a song of each self. Each person's character is expressed not through the acquired or the developed, not through the historic list of accomplishments, but in the limit etched by one's self-presentation. In this limit one finds a remarkable irony: memorable expansiveness encapsulated in the brevity of a Haiku – a ramifying emotional movement that is life lasting.

Let us return to Yip's translations of Chinese poems and to the task of translation in general. I will quote his translation of a Chinese character into a few of its associated words arranged over five lines. The poem is 'Him I'm Thinking Of'[24] and each line is numbered as Yip's text presents them numerically.

9.	in	wind	let-fly	its	ash
10	from	now	on	—	
11.	not	again	of-each-other	think	
12.	of-each-other	think/ thinking	with	you	sever
13.	rooster/cock	crow	dog	bark	

Yip translates these lines as follows:

9.   And let the wind blow its ashes
10.   From now on
11.   No thought of him
12.   No more – the end with him
13.   Cocks crow; dogs bark

As Yip has already pointed out, it is impossible to translate Chinese poems into conventional syntactical forms as he has tried to do here. What is lost is the dream-like movement of words as things-in-themselves. 'In   wind   let-fly   its   ash' creates a very different image from 'And let the wind blow away its ashes.'

Bear in mind, as well, that Yip has translated the characters into single words or pairs of words, when any of these characters would in fact have multiple meanings. Even if we allow that the poet intended the wording that Yip identifies, it would be impossible for such words not to evoke in the Chinese reader the cluster of associations that clings to them. No word can stand alone as it will always link to other impressions created by the single character.

The absence of a speaking voice, the presentation of what seems to be a poem speaking itself without an author – simply stating itself ('of each   think   with   you   sever') gives poetry an *other* reality, strikingly similar to Freud's theory of unconscious thinking.

My reading of Freud's theory of free association argues that each unit of narrative articulated by any patient is simply a condensation of a thousand ideas moving in a dense palimpsest of interlocking impressions, ideas, feelings, urges. Similarly, each Chinese poem is not simply a literary work. Each poem is a *placement* in consciousness of an unconscious process of thought; so that each time it is spoken (or sung or danced to) the speaker enters the realm of unconscious thinking.

It may come as no surprise that while the great thinkers of the East – Lao Tzu, Confucius, Mencius, Zhuangzi – developed the Eastern mind, it is the poets who have demonstrated it. It is not simply that poetry reveals the trials and tribulations of the individual self: the poem *is* the self. Structured, ritualized, mannered and stylized, the poem is the quintessential human reflection of the Eastern mind. As mass society develops in China and human behaviour is codified, people live within the parameters of social metrics and rhythms, rhyming with one another through collective being. In the poem, however, they find their double – a literary Doppelgänger – which obeys all the rules and yet, precisely because of its limitations, finds in the poetic structure room for unique arrangements of common themes.

The private, familial, communal, and mass function of poetry in the East fulfils and integrates the Daoist and Confucian agendas in quite remarkable ways. In discussing the poetry of Valery, Blanchot[25] argues that to write a poem is *to think*, to inhabit the space of thought. 'Art has a goal; it is this very goal. It is not simply a way of exercising the mind; it *is* the mind', he writes. He continues, 'the work is mind, and the mind is the passage, within the work, from the supreme indeterminacy to the determination of that extreme'. It is in the work that we see our mind and 'the mind, then, sees once again in the work only an opportunity to recognize and exercise itself ad infinitum. Thus we return to our point of departure.'

Blanchot paves the way for another understanding of how the poem functions for the Eastern mind. We have discussed how it houses the intimate particularity of individual experience, the privacy of deep emotional experience. We have added now that it is also the place where the mind realizes itself.

The Eastern civilizations revered poems; they collected them by the thousands, and they became, so to speak, the language of the land. We come therefore to the startling conclusion that the Eastern mind seems to have privileged unconscious thinking over conscious thought. It is as if poetry exists as the storehouse of a people's unconscious life. The consciousness of language is borrowed in order for poets and their readers to dive into an unconscious matrix, sharing a canon of common objects that yield deeply private and idiosyncratic meaning. Poetry has been appreciated in the Western world but it has not been put to this use.

The Chinese are explicit about the profundity of poetry as compared with fiction. The Chinese word for fiction is 'small talk' (xiaoshuo) and, as McDougall and Louie point out,[26] their novelists would adopt pseudonyms to avoid the shame of engaging in a denigrated form of verbal trivia.

Nonetheless, in the 11th century the Chinese did begin to write what are arguably the world's first novels.[27] The most famous examples are *Romance of the Three Kingdoms* and *Water Margin* (14th century), *Journey to the West* (16th century) and *Dreams of the Red Chamber* (18th century).

A comparison of the Western and Eastern novel is well beyond the reach of this study, but the literary critic Ming Dong Gu addresses some points of interest. While acknowledging the disparagement suffered by the novel in China (especially at the hands of the Confucians), Ming Dong Gu argues that it cannot be compared to the Western novel because it is subjected to what he terms a process of 'aestheticization',[28] by which he means that narrative fiction eventually simulates lyric poetry. For Ming Dong Gu the poetic enters the Chinese novel and transforms it, so it differs fundamentally from the Western novel and does not threaten the mental function provided by poetry.

Chapter 3

Rites of Passage

Like the *I Ching* and *The Book of Songs, The Book of Rites* (*Li Chi*) was composed over centuries and constitutes a sophisticated index of social behaviour. Legge's deservedly famous translation introduces the reader to the *Li Chi*: 'Confucius said, "It is by the Odes that the mind is aroused, by the Rules of Propriety that the character is established, from Music that the finish is received"'[1] affirming a view that these foundational texts accomplish a seamless task.

If the *I Ching* allows the self to play with the existentiality of human being, if *The Book of Songs* sequesters the soul in poetry, then *The Book of Rites* is a literary boot camp for character formation. Legge dates the first two books of rituals to the Kau dynasty (1122–225 BCE) but points out that it is during the Han dynasty (206 BCE–220 CE) that the previous books are assembled into a more coherent and standard form. *The Book of Rites* continued to be added to – very much in the way the other classical or mother texts are works of social imbrication – and is composed of a sequence of books that address, amongst other things, how and where one should stand in the presence of others, where one should sit at a table, how one should eat, how men and women should behave in one another's presence, how rulers should behave in the presence of the people, how sons should behave in relation to fathers and elders, how long one should mourn and in what manner. It is a seemingly endless, meticulous detailing of behaviour.

Unsurprisingly, being wordy is out: 'one should not (seek to) please others in an improper way, nor be lavish of words'[2] and one should not gossip: 'Let him not appropriate (to himself) the words (of others), nor (repeat them) as (the echo does the) thunder.'[3]

Young men must know what to do with their eyes. When entering a house – only after one has been careful to raise one's voice to announce one's presence and only after hearing voices from within the dwelling – 'when about to enter the door, he must keep his eyes cast down.'[4]

'When two men are sitting or standing together, do not join them as a third'[5] and there are innumerable rules for proper behaviour according to rank, whether meeting someone on the street, dining together or attending social gatherings.

Some of the rites are amusing, such as the suggestion that no one attempt to eat soup with chopsticks, or 'when one sees at a distance a coffin with the corpse in it, he should not sing'. And, conversely, 'when present on an occasion of joy, one should not sigh'.[6]

Although the *Book of Music* has sadly not survived, it is clear that the Chinese loved to sing and dance, so much so they needed to be reminded not to do so at a funeral! Indeed, it would appear that music was generally associated with joy rather than sadness: 'When occupied with the duties of mourning, one should not speak of music'.[7]

Great care had to be exercised upon death. 'When the ceremony of wailing is over, a son should no longer speak of his deceased father by his name'[8] and before entering a house one should ask about the names to be avoided. This did not apply to rulers; one was remitted to speak the names of those mentioned in the *Book of Songs* or the *Book of History* even if they happened to coincide with otherwise prohibited names.

It is impossible to convey the density, range, and thoroughness of the *Book of Rites*. Some of it seems supercilious, other aspects are thick with an over-regulation of the self, some books seem merely concerned with good manners, others are codes of administrative conduct.

And lest it be assumed that there is no Oedipal configuration represented in the Chinese canon, there are unusual restrictions placed upon the eldest son in the filial relation to the father and to elders. Were this not so, argues the book, then men would simply act as beasts. What kind of beasts? 'If (men were as) beasts, and without (the principle of) propriety, father and son might have the same mate.'[9] At which point the writers of *the Book of Rites* come to the kernel of the entire work: 'Therefore' they conclude 'when the sages arose, they framed the rules of propriety in order to teach men, and cause them, by their possession of them, to make a distinction between themselves and brutes'.[10] In other words, the *Book of Rites* boils down to a set of regulations which aim to prevent the sort of mess Oedipus got himself into with Jocasta.

In emphasising ritual as a means of shaping aspects of humanity (8.2)[11] it seems that Confucius was pointing to an intermediate form of knowledge between the maternal and paternal orders. We could say that the axioms taught by the mother are demonstrated through her rituals. They are enacted by her and received by the infant who integrates them into his or her being. Other rituals later demanded of the self by the social order carry with them a different weight from those determined in the maternal order, but even paternal-order injunctions link to the maternal as a supportive matrix.

We can make a distinction between pre-verbal and verbal rituals, between those evolved in mutuality within the maternal order and those imposed during the negotiation of the Oedipal period. However, just as the maternal unconscious does not determine the infant, the paternal order does not construct the post-Oedipal child. Human personality begins as a set of unconscious dispositions prior to any engagement with the other and will be shaped, in part, in opposition to the rituals on offer. Those that Confucius identifies, however, are rituals that a self should elect to adopt as part of a way of living.

For although ritual may at times represent the imposition of fatiguing, rule-bound behavioural directives, it may also replace the presence (in person) of an oppressive, dominating other with the mandate of a set of laws. If the self transforms these laws into more benign, ordered forms of behaviour, and sees that other selves have done the same, then we might say that the *group* triumphs over the primitive law of the father.

In an earlier essay[12] I have argued that the Oedipal complex dissolves through the arrival of the group which obeys not the logic of the father, but the more labile laws of group psychology. In effect, the father is outnumbered.

One question is whether adaptation to ritual dispossesses the true self of that kind of spontaneity that would be evidence of the naturalness-in-being that Confucius also espouses: the way of The Good. In 12.1 The Good is defined as how one lives as the exemplar of goodness.[13] Indeed, he struggles to discover The Good even amongst the highly esteemed. In one sense, his apparent pessimism can be seen as an astute political comment on the corruption of his time: it is more politic to state that no one is Good than to single out the authorities for criticism. He is still faced, however, with a vexing problem. Not only do his teachings seem to be implicit evidence of a failure to internalize the rituals by which the self might be structured but, more critically, the very endeavour to teach people how to behave risks fostering a false self. How could they be natural after what amounts to a rigorous training in adaptation?

It may well be that the split between The Way where one is in harmony with the essence of the universe, and the actual world, in which the self must operate strictly according to learned behaviours, is a split that is cultivated and sustained in post-Confucian society. We live in two worlds. In the first very private realm, cocooned by the self-hypnotic trance of meditation, we find a certain form for our being and relating. A derivative of the maternal order, it is very familiar to us and we do not feel alone when in this state. But it is in marked contrast to the social world of political interaction, in which it is mandatory to learn how to behave in order to avoid corruption, materialism and the lure of ambition and pride.

Confucius sustains this split in his own discourse. One moment he is 'in' the world of The Way, speaking about the universal aspects of being. Another moment he is in the world of the real, addressing an interlocutor and relating a story of human behaviour. Again and again, however, we find Confucius linking the two worlds, bringing the split nature of the self into some form of internal communion. Our natural self, our simple self,[14] uncontaminated by complexity, can filter into the ritualized forms of being like water into a container and imbue the realm of adaptation with a kind of luminous spirituality.

The Chinese way of being, densely ritualized into a collective unconscious, poses interesting psychological issues. In 'The personal and the collective unconscious' Jung argues that, while we have a 'personal unconscious', we also inherit 'impersonal collective components in the form of inherited categories or archetypes.' He suggests that 'it is not a question of inherited ideas, but of inherited thought-patterns.'[15]

Geza Roheim[16] discussed similar thought patterns endemic to the cultures he studied, and Gordon Lawrence[17] has brought a refreshing new theory of collective thinking in his concept of 'social dreaming.' In a social-dreaming group, people come together to tell their dreams and the group discovers how these reflect problems occurring in their work life or in society at the time. Freud certainly does not rule out this possibility in the interpreting of dreams, but his emphasis on personal psychology has tended to exclude social psychology from psychoanalytic dream interpretation.

Reading Confucius, one senses the struggle to communicate 'categories' of being such as 'virtue', 'goodness', or 'the gentlemanly way', that aim to form human beings into collectively shared unconscious assumptions. Within this collective path – The Way – each self lives a life in harmony with the universe which, of course, includes the world of other men and women. The individual exists as a humble presence within the larger order of things, but this position does not invite the subtle pride of humility or submission; it promotes instead a sense of inner freedom that is contingent upon one's state of harmony with the world. If one is part of the group, without personal significance, then 'the internal good' of which Confucius writes becomes a mental dwelling space.

The question of the individual versus the collective, posed in China, is also disseminated through the cultures of Korea and Japan. Of course the issue of the psychic division between self and society is not confined to the Oriental world. From the psychoanalytical perspective, in *The Divided Self*, R. D. Laing elaborates Winnicott's conception of the human being as fundamentally divided between the true and the false self. Laing suggests that the family, and society, drive the schizophrenic into a psychotic split between self and other or self and group. For Winnicott, however, the false self is an ingredient in health, an essential form of protection for the true self which must not be penetrated by the demands of the outside world. For Lacan there is a fundamental alienation between the self in the imaginary order and the self of the symbolic order.

As we have mentioned, the infant-child passes from the maternal into the paternal order and experiences the Oedipal triangle. The first group – the family – constitutes a fourth object, however, which begins to break down the hegemony of the father, whose symbolic power and personal domination cannot assume effective power over the group. This applies both to the family as a group, and more importantly, to the group of ideas forming in each individual self.

The Oedipal self will soon be shattered by the non-familial social group that moves, sometimes in psychotic patterns beyond the organization of self or family.

If we see the Oriental mind as evolving to deal with the potential conflict of self and society, then the Eastern solution would be aiming to find harmonious links between the inner and the outer worlds. Lao Tzu, Confucius, and other philosophers of the 100 year period (4th century BCE) all perceived the hazards of the large group. Daoism brings the group together through mystical unity with the maternal order and Confucius convenes the group around filial identity. These transitional authors (and objects) are well on their way to solving the problem of the integration of private self and public realm.

Part Two

Realizations

Chapter 4

Life's Gate

There is considerable debate about when Lao Tzu lived – some have him living in the 6th century BCE but most writers place him in the 4th century BCE.

He is reputed to have known Confucius and many legends have risen around his name – including one that he travelled to India and taught the Buddha – but there is also some controversy over whether he ever actually existed. Assuming he did, the question of his existence would no doubt have amused him, as much of his philosophy is based on the idea – one of the core axioms of the Oriental mind – that our personhood is a comparatively meaningless particle of the powerful spiritual dissemination of a kind of energy field: 'The Way' or 'Dao'.

Legend has it that when Lao Tzu felt he had had enough of his own country and its society he decided to travel. He came to the Western Gate where he was met by its Guardian, Yinxi. In order to pass he had to prove that he bore some wisdom. He recited what we know as Lao Tzu's *Dao De Jing*,[1] passed through the portal and disappeared. With the *Dao De Jing* we arrive at a mid-point in Chinese thinking. Saturated with the mother texts, it builds upon core mental assumptions – the balance of opposites, the natural and evolutionary nature of events, and the ineluctable fact of change – to find a psychic position for the self within our transient existence.

My reading of the *Dao* will be associative and linked to psychoanalytical ways of thinking. My aim is to indicate how

Lao Tzu and other seminal Chinese thinkers conceptualize a self constituted within the maternal order and how their emphasis on the form of one's living can be as seen as the ancestor of the axioms that underlie the thinking of D. W. Winnicott and Masud Khan, who have built a praxis upon the act that we term 'psychoanalysis'.

When representing the *Dao* I will adopt a prose idiom more in line with its poetic style. When discussing psychoanalysis and Western ideas I do so from a standard style of discourse.

There have been hundreds of translations of the *Dao* and none of the contemporary versions have much in common at all. Rather than elect a single text to cite I have opted to summarize certain passages and on a few occasions I have made my own translation.[2] To fully grasp the links I am making to the *Dao* I recommend that readers find an edition, read the chapters I use, and then proceed to my commentary.

One

Lao Tzu writes that although we may use words such as 'The Way' to name the path we follow in life, words do not describe the 'unnameable'. Even though words arrive out of the experience of that which they name, they are separated from it. The unnameable is the beginning of everything: both mother and infant. The unnameable origin of being is the 'portal to the enigmas' of The Way.

If named, this enigma is 'mother.'

How might one think of this psychoanalytically?

Winnicott believes we are born not as individuals but as part of a unit, fused with the mother and the environment. We begin as pure existence and, if the mother is good enough, a 'continuity of being'[3] is established that allows our 'kernel'[4] (or true self) to arrive through spontaneous actions. This allows us to be in touch with The Way: our true self in song and dance with a transformational and transcendent other.

Our first expressions are bodily as we move about in communication within a maternal sea, a sensational world of water that conducts light, sound and motion. We hear the steady drumbeat of our mother's heart and the voice of her organs. We hear sounds from the world surrounding her, and some of these – such as the voice of the one whom later we shall call Father – become familiar to us.[5]

Psychoanalysis recognizes the trauma of birth. Perhaps as we move with our mother's motions toward the next stage of our being (our birth), we sense something of the ultimate reality. Is the 'portal to the enigmas' the birth gate that delivers us into something beyond foetal imaginings?

Do we remember this?

How could we not?

Might psychoanalysis be part of this remembering?

In English culture, which may for various reasons[6] be closer to such a remembrance, psychoanalysts tend to have consulting rooms that are dimly lit and yet luminous. The rooms are comfortable, with few paintings or physical distractions, so that the self is able to recline into interiority. Rather than using couches most analysts provide an ordinary bed covered with soft quilting and a pillow. Analysts sit behind the patient, out of sight, thus sustaining an illusory sense that both are inside the same object. Winnicott encouraged his analysands to return to a state of 'unintegration'[7] or formlessness.[8] Sometimes his patients fell asleep. Often, so did he.

He wrote of an 'essential aloneness'[9] that precedes our being, of a line running throughout a human life, a continuity-in-being that is visible through vital moments that indicate the kernel of the individual moving forward as a true self. The transition from non-existence to continuity-of-being, he saw as entirely dependent on the self being in the care of a 'good enough mother'. This comes very close to Lao Tzu's emphasis on the role of the mother in constituting the origins of our being.

Two

As soon as we see beauty in the world, we find ugliness. Any object brings up its opposite, so good, for example, elicits the idea of evil. Actions cannot produce their intended outcomes. One finds The Way through inaction.

In psychoanalysis, if one gives the self over to its unconsciousness then one cannot, as a conscious being, claim possession of anything. We abandon preconception, intention and reward. Recognition of our participatory existence does not damage the self, but to claim credit for what is created outside consciousness is damaging, as it presupposes an omnipotence that is not true to being human.

Similarly, Winnicott privileges *being* over *doing*. If the self considers doing things to be the measure of self-fulfilment then it will be at the cost of the self's being. To identify life driven by doing, Winnicott invented the term 'false self',[10] the fundamental duty of which was to protect the true self from invasion.

Ten

Lao Tzu asks if we can participate in The Way without difference, if we can be within it always like a newborn. Can one see without the blight of knowledge? Can one remain open, and especially to the portals through which one passes?

Embracing The Way requires us to recapture the moment in our being when we were at one with our mother. In Twenty Lao Tzu writes: 'I live inside my mother, suckling her milk'. He is making the link between The Way and Union with the mother.

This theory is entirely consistent with the foundation of Winnicott's thinking. Winnicott writes of the feminine element that is in all of us.[11] 'The study of the pure distilled uncontaminated female element leads us to BEING, and this forms the only basis for self discovery and a sense of existing'.[12] The male element is object-relating, backed by instinct and characterized by 'doing'.

Freud, too, recognized that the early ego, the 'primary repressed unconscious', is composed of 'thing presentations',[13] images and impressions from the things of the world before they are re-presented in language. This pre-verbal order is *another* world, one that we leave, not only through acts of separation and development but because the terms of this world are subjected to amnesia. According to the Freudian schema it is a realm we are meant to forget and simply incorporate, because memory of it cannot be sustained through the storage house of language.

Although Freud does not construct a theory of the infant-mother relation, his concept of the primary repressed unconscious as formed by the *impressions* of things certainly opens up an entirely new realm for his metapsychology. It implies that the mother is not only the most important 'thing' in the infant's life, she also presents the object world – thousands of things – to the infant through her actions and the choreography of maternal discourse: her soundings, her touch, her visual presentations, her intuitions.

The imaginings of Lao Tzu are passionate testimonies to the infantile epoch in human being, an era when knowing is through experiencing, when the self is receptive. And, as discussed, he associates this with the feminine. In my own writing I have termed this 'the receptive function of the unconscious' or the 'receptive unconscious',[14] which is a concept markedly different from the Freudian repressed unconscious. Although mental contents certainly can be rejected and repressed by consciousness to exist in resisted exile, there are other parts of the mind that contain wishes, feelings, gratifications and meetings with the world that are not repressed; indeed, they form the matrix of the self's desire.

This kind of knowing begins with the origins of our universe when we are inside the mother and continues most intensely for the first years of our life. We shall always be governed, in part, by our receptive unconscious but never more so than in the early years during when our self is formed. To some extent the receptive unconscious could be likened to Yin, and its active creative counterpart – what I term 'genera'[15] – could be likened to Yang. The *I Ching* emphasizes the need for balance between Yin and Yang, between the receptive and the creative functions of one's being.

Fourteen

Sight, sound, touch, do not reach the intangible and formless essence that is there as Lao Tzu's 'presence of form.' But in a special moment we can see, hear and grasp 'it' even as it is unseen, unheard and unreachable.

Psychoanalytic theory certainly recognizes a mystical period in our lives.

Before language, before the sharing of the image governed by words, all of us are in communion with the indistinct energy of the forms that shape our world. We do not see what 'it' is, which is why I have written that the mother is perceived as a process of transformation, as a 'transformational object.'[16] She is the form behind the form of things. She moves objects, but her authorship of such motion is not visibly detectable except, possibly, through the mystical moments when the infant senses he or she is in touch with the 'maternal origin of all being.'

At certain moments the analysand experiences the form of the formless, as linguistic utterances are undermined and displaced by another set of meanings generated between the phrases of verbal expression. These are the 'tissues of thought' or 'latent contents' that are not explicit, not revealed, but are inferentially grasped as the hidden pattern that resides beneath manifest speaking. Together they form sequential patterns similar to those present in music, in painting, or in any activity that involves a self moving in space and time.

These patterns (the form of our meaning) are the thought-world of the infant and the mother, communicating at levels of unconscious perception that, though unrepresentable and intangible, are the most prescient phenomenon shared between the two. When Winnicott writes that analysis creates a formless state[17] between patient and analyst, or when Masud Khan describes his analysands' regressions to dependence and 'silence as communication'[18] both writers address the world before words and, later, the world between words, when self and other are engaged in different forms of communication.

We have seen how the classical Chinese language – tenseless, without pronouns or syntax, image based – merges the speaker and the listener into the object world. In itself, such a structure sustains the thought world of the self's earliest experiences of life.

Sixteen

'Reach the utmost emptiness.' If still, non interfering, one witnesses the way life, returns to its source – 'to the origins once more'. This is rejuvenating. If one understands The Way it endures through to the end of a lifetime and one need not fear death.

Thinking psychoanalytically, every day is followed by the night. We go off to sleep in order to renew our strength for the following day, but also because we need to dream. To dream is to return to the foetal position, to return to the source from which we emerged to renew our connection with the Primal Mother. To dream over a lifetime is to dream of many lives.

By making space for the dream, psychoanalysis also allows room for two dreamers – the patient and the psychoanalyst – to renew one another's creative vitality. Dreams challenge us again and again and again; night after night after night – the heartbeat of our mind. We remember our dreams, we give them our after-thoughts, and we know that, although we shall never grasp them, they invest us with an intangible knowing that increases our unconscious participation in lived experience.

Twenty One

A person of unique strength values the ungraspable essence of the universe. Unrepresentable, this essence is the origin of creation. It permeates all things and brings us together.

In my writings I have maintained that the kernel of the individual originates with a form of intelligence that operates before the act of conception.[19] This is held within the biology of our species, in our DNA, and it is one of the innumerable forms of intelligence that govern all the structures and actions of the universe.

Although we cannot *think* what we know, we have an endopsychic sense of this thread that courses through our lives and connects us to the other threads that move through existence. If we suspend consciousness or if we enter a state of reverie and are caught by this knowledge, we experience a 'mystical moment' when we sense this essence of our lives.

The repeated act of *psychoanalyzing* establishes a rhythm in which we receive the threads of the other in a state of reverie and allow such patterns to arrive in our consciousness. This process mirrors the act of going to sleep and having a dream, when a particular condition elicits deep news from within our being. But it also creates a link with all the beings who have preceded us, as we discover in this rhythm a movement that connects us with the timeless and the eternal. We enter an ever-present stream. Even when we leave it to re-enter the realm of ordinary human consciousness we retain a sense of that stream. We remember it, not through words, images or any acoustic vocabulary. We remember it as a psychic sensation. It is the realm of the unthought known.

Twenty-Five

The mother of all beneath heaven and earth is beyond our understanding. It is the hand of the universe. It has an 'integral nature'[20] and unifies the world into four realms.

As human selves we are an expression of that creativity from which we are derived and which runs through us. Our being, like all beings, has an integrity that is intangible but also gravitational. It is the *field* of our intangible being that functions within our mind as another form of consciousness that we may think of as super consciousness.

The term super consciousness,[21] to be differentiated from the psychoanalytic superego, derives from an endopsychic awareness, a knowledge that we do not govern our being, that it follows an intelligence (our unconscious) that flows through us and guides the logic of our body, our mind, our life. It is a perspective gained when we are thrown outside of our own narcissistic cluster into awareness of the threads that run through us as beings. During the stream of sessions in a psychoanalysis, which returns the participants to the origins of their birth, to the various stages of their lives, to the logic of body and mind, to the tension-filled wisdom of the limits of conscious knowing, both are dipped in the stream of super consciousness.

Chapter 5

Spiritual Integration

To continue with Lao Tzu.

Twenty-Seven

A good traveller leaves no tracks. A great orator is without speech impediment. An expert on tying leaves no knot.

Those who are wise follow the instructions of gifted teachers.

From a psychoanalytic perspective, one who lives within unconscious thinking is absorbed in thought. Unconscious thinking is any self's creativity. Those psychoanalysts who receive the analysand's creation of their analysis are especially able to help those who are unaware of such creativity. Even if the analysand is intelligent and gifted, if he does not grasp the integrity of the analyst's listening then he will be alienated, not only from the analyst but from his own unconscious life.

Twenty-Eight

It is important to value both the strength of masculinity and the femininity within us. To value the feminine is to take part in the flow of life and one returns to being the newborn babe. If one follows the path one will discover its pattern and one will make patterns.

Psychoanalysis recognizes and uses the masculine principle, which arrives after we have progressed through the early, crucial *formative* period of our lives. Once we have grown into the realm of the paternal order we can look back on the formative period and evoke the integrity of the maternal while employing the discretionary strength derived from the paternal order. We must value the feminine in order to be in touch with the constant nature of the origin of things, especially of our self in its primary being, and to sustain the possibility of the newborn.

Psychoanalysis operates from and between the maternal and paternal orders, which are present simultaneously in the bound and unbound temporality of the analytic hour. The session is time-limited, thus according with the laws of the paternal: father time. But within this bound temporality there are portals through which the self is transported to the infinite temporality of the maternal.

The self moves through the stages of infancy from the paranoid/schizoid to the depressive position, from a fractured sense of being to the infant-wisdom of the world-as-whole, with good and bad contained in a single realm. Then the self discovers the 'integrity of objects'.[1] Each thing – a plant, a bird, a song, a running stream – has its own form, its own structure. To discover this is to comprehend that, although we may animate the object with our own projections, the object is composed of its own features. The carving of a sculpture does not alter the integrity of wood.

Recognition of the integrity of objects allows us to embrace and to be part of the universe of all objects. Our capacity for 'perceptive identification'[2] allows us to play with the passions of projective identification because we know that such play will not annihilate the object.

Perceptive identification is a form of love based on implicit empathy for the qualia of the object, and it is the sign of a self that has its own integrity.

Thirty-Nine

The heavens, the earth, valley, spirits; each achieves oneness and in this way gathers strength.

The idea of integrating one's spirit with the essence of the universe is analogous to integrating the complex unconscious *intent* of a self with what I shall call the *aim-logic* of the universe. Aim-logic refers to the underlying purpose of a logic: the aim of a sequence-in-being. To say that the universe has an aim seems to border on the absurd, unless we borrow from the circumnavigational thinking of Lao Tzu, which says that the aim of the universe is the universe. The logic of its aim is partly evident in what is presently discoverable in the universe, but if that process extends to infinity then the logical unfolding of the aim will never be discovered. It just is.

If this is so, then can we still be in accord with its aim even if we do not comprehend its logic?

In psychoanalysis we might say that the aim-logic of any self is the unfolding of one's being, otherwise known as the development (through being and relating) of one's idiom. If not disordered, then humans will create worlds that integrate with wider (other) worlds and, ultimately, with the universe. Whether disordered or not, in being born and in dying we all exist, in accordance with the physics of reality. But if we *know* this, and if we integrate this awareness into our daily being, then we are working on our own 'subtle spiritual integration.'

Lao Tzu says that when we are confused by events surrounding us we can overcome such distress through 'the strength of the unnameable simple' (thirty-seven). Thinking psychoanalytically we might consider that, although events in our environment can be overwhelming, if we reside within our core self – the integrated structure of our being and the governing law of our relations – we can dissolve the angst arriving out of environmental impingements.

This integrated structure is the form (or personality logic) of our self and Lao Tzu understands this way of being as preceding, and prevailing over, language: 'instruct without speech.'(forty-three). In forty-seven he asserts that we know things best if we never go out of the front door to find knowledge.

He is suggesting that we can know The Way through endopsychic knowledge.

In <u>eighty one</u> he contends that wisdom resides not in what one says, not in what one accumulates, but in the way one lives. For Winnicott, the true self is not a personality feature or a mental content. It is a form of movement. It identifies those moments when one's actions are reflections of a spontaneity that originates from the kernel of the self. As the self-in-movement it expresses the self's pulsations, the interests deriving from the psyche that become shape. These shapes precede the linguistic or the relational but they use words, others and objects to realize form.

In the 1980s I struggled to find a word that could be used to represent the unique form in being that is each individual. I rejected the word 'style' because it implied a generic identity, such as an identifiable fashion of dress or speech. Then I happened upon the term 'idiom', borrowed from linguistics, and in *Forces of Destiny*[3] I wrote about the self as an idiom in being.

It was not until twenty years later that I came across Gordon Allport's book *Becoming* which is subtitled *Basic Considerations for a Psychology of Personality*. Allport was known for his meticulous identification of human traits and is considered to be one of the seminal figures in research psychology. He writes succinctly and poetically on his theory of personality:

> Personality is less a finished product than a transitive process. While it has some stable features, it is at the same time continually undergoing change. It is this course of change, of becoming, of individuation that is now our special concern. The first fact that strikes us is the uniqueness of both the process and the product. Each person is *an idiom unto himself* an apparent violation of the syntax of the species. An idiom develops in its own peculiar context, and this context must be understood in order to comprehend the idiom.[4] [Italics mine]

Allport, like Lao Tzu, speaks to the morphology of self. In emphasizing form before content both aim to convey the priority of our idiom of being over the contents of lived experience. We cannot think our own idiom or that of others that surround us, but as we embody our idiom, as we experience the other's being, we have experience-knowledge of these formations. As such, we have a sense – an extra sense – directed from such idioms and therefore unconsciously perceivable. We can feel the movement of these aesthetics.

The act of psychoanalysis makes both participants into vehicles through which idiom is communicated. Each unconscious intuits from birth (or even *in utero*) that such formal communions are the essence of self-other experiencings. Whatever the analyst or the analysand actually says, the act of psychoanalysis and the analytic relationship will always be derivatives of the unthought known resident in each.

Chapter 6

To the Task Inwardly

If Lao Tzu's *Dao De Jing* is an address offered in order to gain admittance to a foreign land – and its eschewing of personal ambition, gain and militancy would surely be eminently reassuring to the border police – Confucius' *Analects*[1] are sayings that aim more specifically to change man and society. He applies a severe standard to those who aspire to attain The Way, and he assumes a quiet arrogance – no doubt deserved – that elevates him above others.

Unlike Lao Tzu, whose poetry *embodies* The Way, Confucius is a pedant who teaches students how to *find* it. He is more worldly; his sayings abound with examples from the lives of real people. While Dante would populate his inferno with his enemies, Confucius offers lessons to be learnt from those who are held up as exemplars of human weakness.

Most of the themes that run through Lao Tzu's sayings are echoed in Confucius. The simple life is better than the complicated one. Virtue is not to be claimed but to be demonstrated. Living in harmony with the world or the universe is more important than making one's mark as an individual. But Confucius is no mystic; he is concerned with teaching people how to behave in the real world.

Unlike the elusive Lao Tzu, Confucius' personal disposition suffuses his sayings. In 6.3 he laments the death of Yan Hui, whom he clearly admired as the last man who truly loved learning, saying that the world is now bereft of *anyone* with this quality. In 5.27 he says that he has yet 'to meet someone who is able to perceive his own faults and then take himself to task inwardly.' In his commentary on 5.27, Zhu Xi writes that few are aware of making mistakes, and even those who know they have done so lack the ability to engage in self confrontation – 'a necessity', he writes, 'if one is to change oneself.'

Confucius' teachings become acts of inculcation. His commentaries on the lives of men point both to those whose actions demonstrate forms of virtue and to those who fail. These are people whose lives, well known to the people of China, have become allegories of the human personality, of the social world, and of the meaning to be found in lived experience. Through them Confucius addresses an entire nation, and his influence flows through the centuries, through an oral tradition built up around individual lives attached to his commentaries.

Confucius intends to structure the self. Lessons in being and relating, repeated thousands of times and passed from one generation to the next, become axioms for mankind. In 5.25 he tells the story of Zuoqiu Ming who believed that artful wordiness, ingratiation and empty gestures were to be avoided if such behaviours concealed what one truly felt. 'Feigning friendship toward another ... is shameful' he stated. Elsewhere, however, he advocated concealing one's true beliefs in order to respect polity.

The Analects are seminal teachings. They are meant to be remembered and passed down. In Bion's terminology, they will form the preconceptions of future generations like seeds germinating in the self. Eventually these sayings, which from a psychoanalytical point of view we would regard as introjects, or mental objects to which one has some private view, will become structuralized. Instead of remembering a Confucian saying that will help one to change one's behaviour, the self will simply act in accordance with that saying because it has become part of one's being. It is, in other words, a form of inherited learning.

One theme that recurs in Confucius' sayings is the value of ritual as a means of structuring the self. This suggests that the source of any such structure will of necessity have to be imposed. In 'A Discussion of Rites', Hsün Tzu (born 312)[2] offers a psychologically sophisticated argument for the instilling of ritual. He recalls that the ancient rulers disliked disorder and established rituals as a way of ordering people's lives so that they would not waste time in heedless activity but instead find pleasure in a patterned, regulated existence. 'Rites are a means of satisfaction'[3] he says. Hsün Tzu outlines the many rituals one can live by – for example, how the sounds of different bells announce different events. In his mind ritual becomes a kind of 'environment mother' – to use Winnicott's term – that surrounds and supports the self.

Rituals, says Hsün Tzu, satisfy human emotions. Indeed 'when rites are performed in the highest manner, then both the emotions and the forms embodying them are fully realized'.[4] What is the point, he asks, of a period of mourning that lasts three years? 'I reply, it is a form which has been set up after consideration of the emotions involved'.[5] The emotional foundation of rituals, he suggests, are birth and death. There is a temporal logic to rites, one that follows emotional needs. 'Rites trim what is too long and stretch out what is too short', he says.[6] To follow within the logic of ritual is to engage life with what Hsün Tzu terms 'reverent formality'.[7]

By focusing on the habits of man, Confucius engages in a rehabilitation of human character. Like other philosophers of his time, he believes that people are straying from a path once followed in what he considers to be a golden age just preceding his own era. He aims to shame people back to their former – better – selves.

Let us consider these ideas as they relate to the course of human development as understood psychoanalytically. Traditionally it is assumed that the child begins to learn the laws of society during the Oedipal phase. From Freud's point of view this is the time when the child is compelled to think about reality. This confrontation comes in many forms. There is the fact of sexual difference: a boy sees a girl who is without a penis; a girl sees a boy and discovers she does not have one. There is the fact of the primal scene: the father and mother engage in intercourse, which is beyond the child's understanding. The primal scene redefines the maternal vagina from the vessel of the self's birth to the orifice serving parental lust. The fact of reproduction – often introduced by the birth of a rival – indicates that one is not born at the beginning of the universe; the self is the outcome of pre-existent engagement between mother and father. The child is forced to register the reality of paternal and maternal desire.

For Lacan, the acquisition of language may be definitive but it is simultaneously de-centring. Although one 'masters' speech one is also compelled to obey the rules of language that cannot be reshaped according to the whim of omnipotent inventiveness. If the self elects to do this and speaks neologisms, the world will not understand what is being said and will reject the speaker who risks, through this deviation from the laws of the culture, a life lived in a psychotic enclave.

The Oedipal phase, however, is not the only time in the self's early life that rules for being and relating are communicated and internalized. Both Freud and Lacan were paternocentric thinkers who neglected to study the mother's government and the child's place in that polity. In the era of the maternal order the mother conveys to the infant through *action* rather than words pathways to being and to relating. These actions will *impress* the infant but they will by no means govern that self's being, since the infant will bring to these existential lessons his or her own disposition. Some maternal laws will be structuralized, some will be altered by the self in infancy and early childhood to suit the self's idiom, and others will be opposed by anti-maternal axioms.

During these long first three years our unconscious elects those axioms that become the structures of our mind. The process that leads to these axioms are negotiated between ego and self, self and other, self and family, self and culture, to become a matrix of assumptions unique to each one of us.

As we have seen, Lao Tzu's sayings address life lived in the maternal order. His poetic writings are akin to the music of the maternal voice. He aims to reconnect us with our origins and, in a language that signifies its terms, he envelops us in the experience of The Way which is 'The Mother of All Things.'

Confucius guides us in a different intrapsychic period. The Way is already in us but Confucius faces the frustration of finding that man is not following The Way; indeed, no one seems to be learning. In other words, he addresses the Oedipal self, who may once have followed the maternal order – indeed it is resident within all of us – but whose striving, arrogance, duplicity, hypocrisy and vengefulness indicate a defiance of the natural world of the maternal.

If we juxtapose his mentality with that of Lao Tzu, what does Confucius' disposition tell us ? I think he operates from a question. What does the self do *after* the Oedipal awakening, the Oedipal humiliation, the Oedipal battle? After the illusions of pre-verbal childhood are shattered by the realities of family and social life? What does the child do when the fairytales told to him in infancy are revealed as lies? What does she do when she recognizes the contingent nature of human reality?

In a brilliant essay, Ming Dong Gu[8] argues that Confucian China conceals Oedipal conflict (especially the infanticidal and patricidal axes of the Oedipal myth so crucial to Freud's theory of the Oedipus complex) through regressive fragmentation of the self. The Chinese 'resolve' Oedipal conflict by substituting it with 'filial piety' which demands subordination of the self to the dictates of the father. For Ming Dong Gu this means that ultimately the Western and Eastern societies are both patrilineal, although this is concealed in China through defensive retreat into filial piety.

While I find Ming Dong Gu's argument compelling and erudite he runs into the same conundrum faced by all analysts. How much of the pre-verbal structures of a self are indigenous and how much are resident due to a retreat from higher-level functioning?

The Eastern emphasis on form over content inevitably privileges maternal-order thinking even if the content of the formed is composed of defensively distorted patrilineal mandates. And even in a culture suffused with patrilineal assumptions, these will nonetheless be formed first by mothers in their communications with children. They will therefore be revised, at least in part, as essential truths of one's existence rather than laws imposed from outside the self.

So, while I agree with Ming Dong Gu that Confucius (in contrast to Lao Tzu) has moved into the Oedipal period and speaks in the paternal order, the Chinese still rely upon form for communication, or assumptions conveyed early on through behavioural 'scripture'. So the paternal order is itself subsumed under the terms of the maternal order.

I turn now to a poet who contrasts experience itself with the speaking of experience.

In *'Chindallaekkot'* ('Azaleas'), the Korean poet Kim Sowŏl (1902–1934) writes:

> When you go away,
> Sick of seeing me,
> though I die; No, I shall not shed a tear.[9]

What do we do when we feel that (m)other has gone away, sick of 'seeing' our infant self? Do we die? Yes. But Kim Sowŏl rebels against the terms of grief: 'No, I shall not shed a tear'. The child who is abandoned is in a battle to survive, to toughen up the self and not to succumb to the agony of loss.

In 'A Day Long After' Kim Sowŏl writes: 'If you seek me on some day long after, / Then I might say 'I have forgotten'.[10] Each of the poem's stanzas repeats the refrain 'I have forgotten.'

What do we do? We forget. But what is it that we forget? We forget that which *could be recalled.* So we forget the (m)other who abandons us to the new reality imposed by the Oedipal complex. In 'The Road Away' Kim Sowŏl writes:

> Miss you.
> Should I say it,
> I would only miss you more.[11]

Speech – the new world of language – only makes recollection worse. So we do not talk about our loss, to ourselves or to others. We repress the memorable, attached as it is to pain. As Freud teaches, however, once we have acquired language, memory will attach itself to words and henceforth a single word may carry mental pain.

A man who was born and raised in America has parents who are French. His mother is named Inez. When he speaks the word 'mayonnaise' he says, 'myinez.' Unconsciously resident in the word is the quiet and sustained love of mother that survives the censorial eyes of the paternal order.

What we cannot forget, ironically, is that which was never represented in memory in the first place. We cannot forget the innumerable axioms conveyed by maternal actions which formed the ego's structure. These axioms remain within us, they are evoked in the poetry of Lao Tzu and by many moments in life when our being is shaped. Those who practice meditation will testify to the sense gained of living in a different dimension, governed by different principles, accessed by a change in space, time, and mentality. In other words, we go to certain places in order to connect ourselves with the unthought known.

Psychoanalysis is one such space. It is a special form of meditative practice that allows the self's axioms to emerge within the transference. The analysand brings the unthought known into presentation by *using* the analyst as an object through which to articulate the self's idiom. Winnicott believed this 'use of the object'[12] had to be 'ruthless'[13] but he was careful to point out that such use did not imply exploitation. Use, in this sense, could only take place if the object (the analyst-other) accepted his or her status as an object of thought and use, knowing that this was a valuable recreation of the world in the interests of true self experiencing. It would be predicated on the earlier period of object-relating, during which primitive negotiations between the elements of the infantile self (love, hate, greed, envy, reparation) were repeated and repeated until the process of maternal holding and containment led from the paranoid/schizoid order to the depressive position. Object usage could then take place because the self had learned that, although the other rejects exploitation, it welcomes usage.

For Winnicott, this use of the object world constitutes the freedom needed for character expression. For Freud, on the other hand, freedom resides in the uncensored speech of the free-talking analysand.

Confucius ennobles the man of virtue who proves through the form of his being rather than the content of his speech that he is an authentic self. Throughout the 'Legalist period' (during the Warring States era) China had to organize a huge community. Laws became binding and Confucius expressed fury with those corrupt individuals who, through their false teachings and edicts, diminished the Han Period which ordered China and which he himself idealized. His commentaries, reflecting the prevailing Chinese ethos, mistrust the free-speaking individual who, through the decentring power of verbal discourse, threatens the collective will to cultivate a mass society.

This tension between individuality and the need to fashion an ordered community is part of the mentality that China brings to the modern world. We can appreciate, therefore, how the aspect of Freudian analysis that privileges the speaking subject – that reveres, indeed, the self that *mis-speaks* – is likely to be anxiety-provoking to the Eastern mind.

In a sense, free associations repudiate conscious assertions and subvert authority. As De Mente points out,[14] although there is a word for 'no' in Chinese, Korean, and Japanese, the word is rarely used. He argues that the population's fear of offending those in authority led to a tendency to avoid any form of assertive statement. One would not want to be held accountable for what one has said. Over the centuries it has therefore been considered impolite to speak bluntly. The Eastern mind prefers to express itself in vague and ambiguous ways, conveying a view to the listener without being direct.

De Mente also points out that the Western mind employs the binary form of 'why' / 'because', a discourse that expects dialogue to be immediate and precise. Because of the view, sustained from the 17th to the 20th century CE in the Chinese Imperial Court, that all questions had been answered, the Western cause-effect questioning would have been considered counter-traditional and therefore offensive.

If Lao Tzu attends to the privacy of the true self and Confucius to the formation of a constructive false self, we may see in the long, slow, evolution of these two philosophies an integration within the Eastern mind of the deeply private and emotional with the social and the restrained.

In Winnicott's praxis we see something of the same integration. While it is true that he fosters regression to dependence in order to promote the freedoms of the true self, he also defends the false self as its necessary protector. Although he does not attend explicitly to the politics of false-self existence, we might say that as a remarkably polite, ordinary English eccentric, Winnicott embodied the conventional forms of his own culture.

Even as the Chinese mind and the mentalities of Winnicott and Khan may, in part, retreat from Oedipal warfare and the violent trajectories of self development, speech, and confrontation with others, such dispositions nonetheless derive from (and may return to) a maternal world based on fusion between self and other, empathic attunement rather than speech, and form-language rather than linguistic discourse as a means of being-together.

Repressed Oedipal contents are always available for de-repression and emergence, but if they have been re-formed through defences, and if those defences have been structuralized in the maternal order, then the forms of the regressive defences will have become part of the self's (or culture's) character and they will remain as habits of life.[15] It is important to distinguish between the content of the conflict (let us say the urge to kill the father and the anxiety over castration) and the form taken to defend against the conflict (let us say being altruistic). Aggression and anxiety may be repressed through altruistic defences but over time, or more pertinently if those forms are passed on to other generations, then the form – altruism – may become independent of its original aim.

The maternal and paternal orders integrate through and within the structure of family life. Hall and Ames argue that 'the family serves as a pervasive metaphor for social, political, and even religious relations within the Confucian world view.'[16] The non verbal forms communicated by the mother in the infant's first encounters meet with the verbal laws enunciated by the father. The unsaid meets with the said, and through time and family culture (the idiomatic way in which each family – and the child experiencing this family – integrate the two orders) a new order is constituted. For Hall and Ames, *The Analects* state 'explicitly that the way of conducting oneself most productively as a human being emerges out of the achievement of robust filial relations', and they quote Confucius: 'As for filial and fraternal responsibility, it is, I suspect, the root of authoritative conduct.'[17]

The family, then, as discussed becomes a fourth object,[18] one that moves beyond the Oedipal triangle and transports the self into a world re-formed by family styles and laws. As we shall see, however, not even the family will serve as the ultimate paradigm for the self facing its future and the large group that we nowadays call a nation.

Chapter 7

Inaction Happiness

Zhuangzi[1] (369–286 BCE) is considered, along with Lao Tzu, Confucius and Mencius, to be one the four great Chinese philosophers. As with them, the sayings attributed to him are likely to be the work of many writers, over centuries, who were inspired by him, so in referring to his work we refer to the work of many. This would no doubt have both pleased and amused Zhuangzi who said 'name is only the guest of reality'.[2] In 'Discussion on Making All things Equal' he contrasts the spirited life of men in their dreams with the humdrum incarceration of their daily lives. 'They drown in what they do ... they grow dark, as though sealed with seals'[3] until they die.

Our affects – joy, grief, regret – are the 'music from empty holes' that spring up like mushrooms in damp darkness and attach themselves to the human form. What Master do they follow? What is the logic of these elements of the human being?

'Once a man receives this fixed bodily form, he holds on to it, waiting for the end'.[4] Throughout his earthly existence, man battles with others, he tears through his life with dumb force, exhausted, bathed in the sweat of his exertions, but taking solace in the fact that he is not yet dead. 'Man's life has always been a muddle like this'.[5]

And yet man has a mind. Why allow the mind to be formed by the axioms of this world before you have sought a teacher? Why not learn about the mind so that it can initiate change? To make demands in the world and to claim to know right from wrong is to proceed without having a mind; it is like saying that what doesn't exist, exists. Like saying that one has a mind when one does not.

In this state, our words are merely wind. 'Words have something to say', but only if we follow The Way. Otherwise they signify nothing. Without understanding the value of words our points of reference are gone. 'Everything has its "that"; everything has its "this"'.[6] If we have not discovered right from wrong these distinctions are impossible.

Each of us has a beginning. But our beginning is not our birth, not at the moment of our being, not at the moment of our nonbeing. 'There is a not yet beginning to be nonbeing'.[7] Then there is the sudden arrival of being; a separation between being and nonbeing. 'Now I have just said something', writes Zhuangzi, 'but I don't know whether what I have said has really said something or whether it hasn't said something.'[8]

Ni Que is asking Wang Ni how he knows that he is naming things correctly. Wang Ni replies: 'What way do I have of knowing that if I say I don't know something I don't really in fact know it?'[9] Zhuangzi asks: 'How do I know that loving life is not a delusion?'[10] and, like Western philosophers, he uses the dream as foil to our sense of reality. 'While he is dreaming he does not know it is a dream, and in his dream he may even try to interpret a dream. Only after he wakes does he know it was a dream. And some day there will be a great awakening when we know that this is all a great dream'.[11]

In Zhuangzi's writing one finds a brilliant and moving blend: a rigorous demand for lucid thinking combined with a clear sense of the unfathomable nature of human experience. 'Is there such a thing as supreme happiness in the world or isn't there? Is there some way to keep yourself alive or isn't there?'[12]

These same questions preoccupied European existentialists such as Albert Camus, who found in the human condition an impossible double bind. To think is to know that thinking does not alleviate our recognition of the absurd nature of our being; indeed, we see this more clearly by thinking than by not thinking. Not to think is to sink into the abyss of negation, to avoid one's obligation to face the truth of one's being, to see it for what it is, to face the absurd and not to blink. But who would want to do this?

Intriguingly, Zhuangzi finds an answer to the dilemmas he poses. While many people live 'life in company with worry' until 'dull and doddering', in answer to the question, 'In the end is there really happiness or isn't there?' he replies, 'I take inaction to be true happiness'.[13]

One finds here a strong echo of Lao Tzu and a chime from Confucius, but Zhuangzi's confrontation of life and the dilemma it poses seems more clear-headed, less idealized and more courageous than that of those philosophers who preceded him. It is against the tapestry of the humdrum, the paralyzing effect of the everyday, that Zhuangzi urges others to find contentment in 'inaction.'

There no evidence that Winnicott ever read Zhuangzi or any Chinese writers; indeed his wife Clare stated that he hated philosophy and only ever enjoyed fiction, which the two of them would read to each other at night before going to bed.[14] However, in the 1950s Winnicott embarked on an experiment in psychoanalysis that would seem to echo aspects of Eastern thinking.

Listening to his analysands, he found that almost all that was said was 'chatter' – the clutter of minds taken up with an over-adaptation to reality. In his view, each person possessed a true self but it was not possible to find a way to that true self by listening to patients' daily accounts of their lives. He believed that free association was an obstruction,[15] producing a thread of ideas that was merely an act of defensive omnipotence and a sign of anxiety.

Winnicott's experiment was to ask (or more emphatically to tell) his patients to be quiet. For some this would come as a shock and at times, no doubt, his confrontations could be brutal. He is reported to have told one patient 'you are only a mouth' and some of his analysands say they felt 'destroyed',[16] even as they sang his praises as a clinician.

Classical analysts had, until Winnicott's time, remained largely silent – imposing a state of abstinence – in order to promote latent anxieties in the analysand that would intensify under the austere terms of psychoanalysis. With no response whatsoever from the other, the human subject would begin to break down. Silence, in other words, could come close to torture.

If the classical model used silence to force the anxious self into fragmentary speech, Winnicott proposed an opposite paradigm, one in which silence became the main medium of analysis. The patient could remain silent for days, weeks or months and there were no transferential expectations. For Winnicott, silence was the language of the earliest state of being; it represented a funda- mental condition of human subjectivity.

Many people sought analysis with Winnicott in order to abandon false self presentations, hoping they would find in his care the means towards a therapeutic regression. Of the four psychoanalysts analysed by him with whom I have discussed his technique in some detail, two felt that he had saved their lives. They readily abandoned free associative talking and sank into the holding environment that Winnicott termed his 'formless state.' In such a state the analysand was 'in care' and in a state of 'absolute dependence.'[17]

Having inherited a few of his analysands I discovered that they expected a clinical space that sanctioned long periods of silence unpunctuated by analytical comment. Verbalizations were more like body-mind presentations and it was not possible – or even inviting – to comment.

Winnicott's view was that in the course of development many people had to assume a pathological false self in order to deflect excessive maternal or environmental impingement. They constructed defences that resulted in a heavily fortified personality that aimed almost entirely at reactive living rather than true being. That continuity of being that Winnicott felt was instrumental in the evolution of the infant's true self, that would eventually endow the child with a sense of 'inner personal reality' and lead to 'personalization', had failed to take place. Psychoanalysis offered a temporal, spatial and relational idiom that allowed for a dissolution of the false self and, through primitive dependence on the analyst, there would be the gradual emergence of true-self states out of formlessness. If, that is, the silence of the analysand was viewed not as a resistance but as a matrix of communication with the analyst.

Winnicott's praxis has been likened to a sort of Zen. Indeed it could be said to be a form of post-Daoist practice. One can see in his antipathy to speaking something of the fiercely held Chinese attitude toward speech as wasteful and insincere, and later to the Zen guru's mind-numbing attack on the novice through the *koan*. In a formless state the analysand is without ambition, without aim, without effort, as the complex interferences occasioned by the burden to relate to the analyst are abandoned. Patient and analyst both refrain from ordinary speech and live within a near-silent realm in which the common audible sounds are those of stomachs gurgling, legs crossed and uncrossed, a throat clearing, the rattle of a tea cup on a saucer, bird song, the sound of an analyst sleeping. Like Daoism and Zen, Winnicott's praxis is not a means to an end: to accomplish it is enough.

Analyst and analysand therefore return to a form of sensational living not present since the early years of life. Both may doze off... time will be suspended. Sometimes sessions run over by a few minutes, sometimes they last several hours.

Out of formlessness an image will arise. In a Freudian analysis an image is a concentration of possible words. Speaking will unpack the image, as words express latent meanings with a chain of signifiers. In a Winnicottian analysis the image arrives out of nowhere, seemingly from outside the self. It is a moment in time. It carries weight, yet it is evanescent and without articulated significance. It is not to be spoken, as to do so would be to recognize its separateness from the self. In fact, image and self seem to be in-mixed with one another: the image powerful as a force of the true self arriving out of nothingness. The analysand thus experiences the innate and spontaneous construction of his own being emerging out of liminal interludes of non being.

When Winnicott did speak it was often simple and declarative. 'You are inside your mother'. 'You are where you lost your being.' 'Your mother's death is present.' By avoiding discursive discourse, speech becomes a thing, like the image. Image and word both bear an enhanced similarity to the real, as if both imaginary and symbolic orders have been subordinated to a different order of transmission.

Winnicott's clinical technique, with its brief verbal shocks, is in striking contrast to his extended clinical writings in which he provides schematic and wordy 'reconstructions' of his patients' histories.

Otherwise, when writing about the theory, his writing has a brevity and poetic quality frequently noted by fellow analysts, sometimes with frustration. At a meeting of the British Psychoanalytical Society, Winnicott famously said, 'There is no such thing as a baby.' He paused while his audience silently gasped. How could the world's greatest paediatrician say something like this? Then, in one of the most famous moments in the history of psychoanalytical poetics, he added '... without a mother.' Winnicott, who invented games to play with infants, knew how this statement would accomplish an emotional effect that more prosaic expression could never achieve.

He viewed psychoanalytic interpretation more as a poetic action than as a pedantic moment. 'My interpretations are economical, I hope. One interpretation satisfies me ... I say one thing, or say one thing in two or three parts. I never use long sentences unless I am very tired.'[18]

It was Winnicott's analysand, Masud Khan, who developed the verbal economy of Winnicott's technique. Khan would speak to his patients in brief, spontaneous, poem-like utterances. Often, what he said would arrive out of the blue as transient evocative utterance with no dialogical intent. They often seemed enigmatic but were emotionally redolent and full of ramifying unconscious meaning.[19]

To Winnicott's practice, Khan added a distinctly poetic dimension. He spoke in aphorisms, sometimes in verse (usually Persian) but more often in short, thickly evocative, imagistic sentences that were intended to word feelings. Language was not being used to explicate matters, or to interpret either the self's internal world or to interpret the analytic relationship. Like Lacan, whose inventiveness he admired, Khan spoke as though to speak was to present the 'thing' of emotional reality itself: a voice of the unconscious with no obvious connection to anything in particular. When the comments were directed to the analysand they were imaginative wordings of the patient's state of being. His words, though transient and without apparent rhetorical aim (such as requesting a reply), were so vivid that they echoed in the analysand's mind long after the session.

Unlike the Zen master[20] who poses riddles that challenge the mind, Khan spoke 'truths' resident in immediate experience. They emerged from the palimpsest of emotional experience: alive in images, bodily experiencing, silences, and feelings between the two selves. By combining these various states into a brief comment, Khan seemed to objectify a moving matrix that carried consciousness like a raft riding a powerful stream. His speech accepted a self's liminality and gave time to the articulation of the unsaid through silences and body states, intrinsic side-effects of the evocative nature of his wordings.

Although Khan's personal behaviour[21] outside the consulting room has provided many a vicarious thrill for the sequestered profession of psychoanalysis, his behaviour within his practice was usually highly disciplined, and his approach generated a medium for occasional epiphanies of knowing that could not have been realized in a more verbally active medium. His capacity for brief, elliptical, poetic statements seemed second nature to him, but no doubt it resulted from the many thousands of hours he had spent developing a praxis that had its own unconscious logic and idiom.

It was the infant-mother relation that provided the paradigm for the form of clinical practice favoured by Winnicott and Khan. A predominantly silent world with occasional quiet, brief, dream-like utterances, does indeed echo the way a mother will speak to a small infant. Unconsciously she supports his going-on-being with the song of the human voice as she gathers into brief statements moments of immediate experience, converting them into an expressed mutuality. It relates especially, perhaps, to the way a mother attends to a small child at night. As he is drifting off to sleep, occasionally needing the reassurance of the parent's voice, she instinctively offers something syntonic with the state of drowsiness, the transitional state of a self moving from wakeful life to the world of dreams.

In a Winnicottian analysis consciousness takes a back seat to spontaneous living, and this arrives out of a lessening rather than a heightening of self awareness. The self's experience-in-being *is* the analysis. In the Freudian model, on the other hand, the analytic process is a medium for the transmission of unconscious contents to both participants, so that each may comprehend something of the analysand's unconscious life. In a Freudian analysis consciousness is raised and this includes a heightened understanding of the origins of the self's conflicts and the nature of the self's problematic psychodynamics and character disturbances.

The premise of a Kleinian analysis is different again. Here the transference is understood as a theatre that houses the self's projection of its psychic structure into mental representations of the analyst and of other objects that may, in fact, also turn out to be derivatives of the analyst. What the patient says is therefore translated systematically into another frame of reference: his statements are understood as encrypted messages about the self, the analyst, and the analytic relationship – all ultimately echoes of the self's psychic history.

In a Winnicottian analysis the transference is understood very differently, as a form of unconscious articulation through object usage. It is as though the self learns and employs a new language in order to speak phenomena that have hitherto been unrepresentable. The Winnicottian lives therefore *within* the form of the transference as an expressive idiom, largely unconcerned with the themes revealed through associative mental contents.

The Kleinian's translation of the patient's narrative into the self's projections reveals a dense, interlocking network of self-interpretations derived from primitive instincts, persecutory anxieties, depressive recognitions, and the complex panoply of defences employed to conceal meaning from the self. The Winnicottian approach reveals no such knowledge. The analysis restages the self's origins, a period when self–other relating was less a matter of internal mental representation and more a reality of self–other experiencing. By returning the analysand to this primary being, 'basic faults'[22] can be healed through the medium of the transference. Winnicottian analysis fosters a memory of a profound experience too ineffable and unthinkable for words to bear. It is, therefore, as fragile a truth as those posed by Lao Tzu or Zhuangzi.

In 'Playing: the search for the self', Winnicott writes that 'the person we are trying to help needs a new experience in a specialized setting.'[23] It is the experience of a 'non-purposive' environment in which the personality is 'ticking over' in an unintegrated state of 'formlessness'. From this vantage point free association, as discussed earlier, is seen as too intentional an act, interfering with the terms of this specialized setting: 'According to this theory, free association that reveals a coherent theme is already affected by anxiety, and the cohesion of ideas is a defence organization.'[24] The evenly suspended analyst open to free association is clearly not the figure Winnicott intends to occupy this setting. 'An opportunity for rest has been missed because of the therapist's need to find sense where nonsense is. The patient has been unable to rest because of a failure of the environmental provision, which undid the sense of trust.'

Winnicott's barely concealed irritation with what he regards as the destructive intrusiveness of Freud's 'basic rule' of free association is driven by his devotion to returning analysand and analyst to a time before words carried meaning: to the frame of mind which he terms 'primary maternal preoccupation'.[25] This refers to the new mother's state of deep devotion to her infant in which both communicate instinctively what they sense, know and desire.

As discussed, In *Playing and Reality* he writes: 'In these highly specialized conditions the individual can come together and exist as a unit, not as a defense against anxiety but as an expression of I AM, I am alive, I am myself. From this position everything is creative.'[26] Such creativity is not the work of integration, but of allowing the unintegrated to form an internal matrix that generates creativity. Writing of a patient in analysis, he states: 'She had now made the essential interpretation in that the question arose out of what can only be called her creativity, creativity that was a coming together after relaxation, which is the opposite of integration.'[27]

When Lao Tzu writes of the simplification of self, of finding through the abandonment of complexity an underlying truth that joins one up with The Way, he heralds a form of cure for the personal ailments of living. This accords with what Winnicott terms 'creativity' – within the self, between self and other, and in the world.

In life we can attempt to find The Way, but we may succumb instead to the material, to corruption, or to a false sense of accomplishment. Confucius translates the *I Ching* and the concept of The Way into a powerful ethical system that blends individual and social harmony. It is possible over time to inculcate forms of being that will be homologous with social forms. This may seem like a means of producing selves that are ritualized to the point of regimentation, but it actually aims to free the self to become participant in the various potential forms that await in the environment: those of the family, the village, the region and the nation.

During the Period of the Three Kingdoms (220–280 CE), and especially in the Koryo dynasty (918–1392 CE), two different notions of form are threaded through Korean neo-Confucianism and the integrations of Buddhist doctrine. Neo-Confucian form is an ethical system of personality development that follows the philosophical and political inclinations to create a virtuous man. In Buddhism, on the other hand, we find (amongst many theories of the self's form) the concept of *kharma*, which is based on the notion that the self has lived a prior life. In other words, that the self has existed in another form.

Recollection of that previous existence and intimations of how one might be incarnated in the next life would not appear to have an obvious analogue in psychoanalytical theory. For Freud, the fact of childhood amnesia erases the memory of this period from our minds. It is no longer within us. However, by sidelining Freud's analytic technique of discovering meaning through free association, Winnicott develops an approach that does indeed return the self to a previous life – the life of infancy. In doing so, he suggests that infantile amnesia must surely be incomplete; there must be some memory of the preverbal era. Winnicott relies, then, on the continuation in the adult of *a sense* of the earlier life, one that cannot be evoked by recollective remembering but can be summoned by a change in self-state, in which the phenomenology of infantile being is elicited through derivative forms. So when we suspend a search for meaning and listen instead to the harmonies of self and other, when we can experience in the play of light a visual pageant of prefigurative images, or when we live within our body-self as we swim, run or dance, we do have intimations of a former self.

What kind of 'other' is Winnicott, then, as the one who attends to the analysand's return to a past life? I do not mean what kind of figure he represents in the personal, regressed experience of the analysand. I mean what kind of other does he propose the analyst to be as the guardian of this form of time-travel? Who would both live in the present and have the capacity to transport the self back to its origins? Remember, Winnicott does not propose that his position is that of a *symbolic* mother in the transference. By presuming to reconjure the conditions that prevailed in the past, his technique supports the recreation of 'the fact' of dependence. His couch is a time-machine.

Winnicott, Khan, Michael and Enid Balint, Nina Coltart and others privileged silence as the communicative medium of the analytic relationship, which facilitated the arrival of emotional experience in the presence of the other. Apparently without knowing it,[28] they therefore created in a psychoanalytic context a form of 'inaction happiness' that corresponds to aspects of The Way. In other words, through their praxis the 20th century analyst was unconsciously assimilating an ancient Eastern frame of mind.

The Winnicottian analysand will not have been psychoanalyzed, at least not in the traditional sense of that term. I do not think that Winnicott was interested in the analysis of psychic conflict, Oedipal structures, projective processes and so forth.

The analysand will instead have been participant in a devolutionary process, lost in the form of the experience. This is the aim of this type of psychoanalysis. The analyst is therefore a *transformational object*,[29] experienced as the guardian of the process and ultimately identified with it.

Valuable and profound as this aspect of a psychoanalysis may be, it is not difficult to see its limitations. If it returns ailing souls to the origins of their basic fault, there to undergo a process of character transformation that renews a sense of personal authorship of their lives, then that is a remarkable change. But such an analysis does not value insight into the self. With speech viewed as a symptom of false self-relating rather than as evidence of true self-presence, the Winnicottian analysand eventually abandons talking about his self, his life and his past. This means that the psychoanalyst gains very little information about the analysand's internal world or active psychic life. In fact the Winnicottian technique constitutes a double bind that actually forbids traditional psychoanalysis from taking place.

With his very different character, I believe that Khan experienced more than his mentor the frustrations of this psychoanalytic double bind: to speak the self but not to use language in so doing. It is, perhaps, the fate of the student to inherit the flaws of the master and to live with the pain of unthought-through contradictions. Khan certainly followed Winnicott's technique in fostering regression to dependence as the *sine qua non* of the analytical experience, but he was a highly verbal, inquisitive and somewhat impatient man. He ordained that the analysands must abandon talking but, just as it deprived them of the verbalization of their lives, this left the curious part of him excluded from their inner worlds. Khan was well known to lament that his patients were all 'unanalyzable' but a question arises as to whether he ever connected his own praxis to that inevitable outcome. How could one be analyzable if the self was discouraged from speaking?

This conundrum is found in other forms in China, Korea and Japan. East Asian cultures inherit and sustain a profound valuing of the non-verbal dimensions of human being, but at the same time they are complex societies that require increasingly sophisticated forms of communication. Competing ideas from the outside world, and especially, perhaps, the blatantly cognitive incursions of the IT age, challenge both the neo-Confucian world of an enclosed ethic, a framed existence that relies on collective agreement, and the Daoist and Zen ideal of generative solitude.

Part Three

Conceptualizations

Chapter 8

Cultivation

In one of his final works, *Exposition of the Vajrasamadhi-Sutra* (*Kumgang Sammaegyong Non*, translated as *Book of Adamantine Absorption*),[1] the great Korean commentator Wŏnhyo (617–686 CE) exhaustively outlines all the elements that go into human enlightenment. His work is far too complex for us to discuss here, but one of his lines of argument is directed towards the elimination of unproductive thought.

The Sutra postulates two fundamental states of mind: 'the true-thusness' (*chinyo/zhenru*) and 'production-and-extinction' *(saengmyol/shengmie)*. Those who are misguided can find enlightenment through the abandoning of false ideas. Contemplation may aim at the destruction of delusion, but the deluded mind engaged in contemplation will continue to delude itself. 'Consequently' writes Wŏnhyo 'one must annihilate all productions of mind. Therefore, the ... approach of contemplation practice ... elucidates the practice of nonproduction'. 'Once one's practice has stopped producing anything', he continues, 'one then experiences original enlightenment'.[2]

This idea brings to mind Winnicott's theory of the elimination of the mind-as-false-self. Destruction of the false self requires the speaking self to be abandoned. Only then can the person return to a position in which the stirrings of the true self (original enlightenment) are possible. As discussed, in *Playing and Reality*[3] Winnicott writes: 'it is creative apperception more than anything else that makes the individual feel that life is worth living', but he contrasts this with 'the relationship to external reality [which] is one of compliance, the world and its details being recognized but only as something to be fitted in with or demanding adaptation'.[4]

Winnicott juxtaposes two features of mental life – the creatively apperceptive and the adaptive – and his psychoanalytic technique aims to suspend the adaptive work of the mind in order to provide a potential space for spontaneous creativity. When an analyst is quiet he does not impinge on the patient, especially if he suspends the demand for free association. Adaptation is unnecessary as nothing is expected. The adaptive mind (false self) therefore ceases to function and this, according to Winnicott, elicits a state of formlessness.

Although Winnicott only rarely makes an explicit challenge to other analytic stances (such as when claiming that he had learned to make few interpretations) he sets out a view of psychic change very different from any that preceded it, and, as we have seen, both his theory and his practice constitute a profound rejection of the verbal side of classical psychoanalytic tradition.

In *Secrets on Cultivating the Mind*,[5] written between 1203 and 1205, the Korean Buddhist poet and philosopher, Chinul, tells us that, 'if you want to become a Buddha, understand that Buddha is the mind'.[6] His concept of mind is close to Winnicott's true self, to some pure essence of being that precedes and authorizes human behaviour. Like Winnicott,[7] he states that the original mind is formless – 'This "formless thing" is the dharma-seal of all the Buddhas; it is your original mind'.[8] Although there are two paths to spiritual enlightenment – sudden awakening and gradual cultivation – the aim is to achieve 'numinous awareness', a mind that is 'pure, void, and calm'.[9]

This awareness may not arrive in a flash. In recounting a tale told by Kuei-Feng, Chinul writes that we may awaken to the fact that the ordinary man is Buddha, just as we note that the mind is like free-moving water, but if the water is frozen in a lake it will take time for the sun to melt it, to free it. Time must pass before a mind can be set free.

Just as Confucianism had provided a counterpoint to Daoism, cultivating the establishing of the thoughts and behaviours required to foster the social self, Zen arose in China, Korea, and Japan as a corrective to the adaptive formalities of neo-Confucian mandates. Buddhism matriculated into China in the first century CE and gradually became the dominant religion. Taking into account that neo-Confucian thought sought its own integration with Buddhism, there was still a clash between the focus on ethical social harmony resident in Confucianism and Buddhism's religious imperative to abandon the ways of the world in order to be enlightened.

This tension between two profound traditions must surely have become internalized within the mental structures of the Chinese, Koreans, and Japanese, who are faced today with the psychic residues of the conflicting schools of thought that have inhabited their thought-patterns for centuries. In the psychoanalytical world, too, we can see a correlation in the tension between the Winnicott praxis and almost all other techniques, most notably Freudian and Kleinian. Psychoanalysis, too, is confronted with the task of comprehending its own resident polarities.

Reading the East Asian literature, we may ask: where is the ordinary mind or the ordinary self to be found? From Lao Tzu, Zhuangzi, Confucius and Mo Tzu to Mao Zedong in China, and in the writings of Wŏnhyo and Chinul in Korea, we find a preoccupation with the ideal self. The Eastern tradition sees everyday human mentality as an impediment to achieving a pure, virtuous, socially harmonious life. Man therefore needs the rehabilitative formations of Daoism, Confucianism or Buddhism if he is to avoid self-dissolution, social disarray or collective disease.

The Eastern ideal is a state of mindlessness. A mind without content is an open mind, available for communion with the formless energy of The Way or the spirit of the Buddha.

Negative qualities such as corruption, idleness and pride are acknowledged as the opposites of the ideal self, but the moralism intrinsic to these writings precludes the development of a psychological literature. What is missing in the Eastern tradition is any substantial recognition of, or interest in, what in the Occidental world would be considered ordinary mental conflict.

Western culture assumes that the self is in perpetual conflict. Beginning with the depth psychologies of the Athenian golden age (Aeschylus, Sophocles etc.), surviving in the religiously inspired *Confessions* of Augustine and transformed by the insightful genius of Shakespeare, this awareness has given rise to the deep interiority of novels and plays that study human minds and human conflict. And it is this traditional Western preoccupation that is reflected in Freud's theory of mind.

We have seen in Winnicott's approach striking parallels to the axioms that govern the Eastern view of mental life and mental health. But it would be akin to an act of negative hallucination to construct a model of psychoanalysis purely around the assumptions and the practices advocated by him, since they are predicated on a radical sidelining of speech, conflict and the thinking mind – in other words, the basic ingredients of classical Freudian psychoanalysis.

We come therefore to a question. Could there be a line of thinking that could link and make meaningful the apparent contradictions between the Oriental mind and the Western world of psychoanalysis ?

What if the mind is fundamentally composed of two opposing forms of thinking, being, and behaving? What if that composition of mind has been transmitted over centuries in the collective unconscious and inherited by each generation? And what if, by reconciling Winnicott's vision with that of Freud, the practice of psychoanalysis – a process that follows the maternal order combined with a technique of interpretation and theories of development derived from the paternal – can offer an integration of these two ways of being and thinking ? What if the model of the self without mind and that of the self preoccupied with intrapsychic conflict could be brought into harmony without eliminating one another?

Lao-Tzu and Confucius are well aware of the nefarious behaviours of mankind. However, seen from a psychoanalytical point of view, it is as if they retreat in the face of the post-Oedipal self to seek in the maternal order a solution to the violent sides of human behaviour. By returning to this maternal order, which precedes speech, they find in the sentient harmony of the infant-mother relation a form of being that becomes the model for human existence. These writers may spend time discussing the world of politics, society and leadership, but their fundamental aim is to neutralize the Oedipal through the eradication of the paternal order. Winnicott's theory and practice likewise give a central place to the prelapsarian world of the infant and mother, the world before the Oedipal fall which shatters toddlerhood with the powerful toxins of envy, rivalry and hate.

In the East a leader is meant to be the exemplar of form, the human embodiment of a principle that he is privileged to demonstrate. Any ruler can fall from grace, but there is always a proper path to which he can return. This charting of the maternal order, meticulously outlined by Confucius, Mencius and others, is probably the most thorough program for a life from cradle to grave that has ever been proposed.

In some respects, Zen thought provides a remarkable back-up for the Confucian order. What if the world seems to be going off the rails? What if, even within an ethical system composed of such prescriptive simplicity, the unruly and destructive sides of human nature still prevail? What if the environment-mother, expanded into the family, school, community and nation – to invoke Yeats 'cannot hold; / Mere anarchy is loosed upon the world / The blood-dimmed tide is loosed, and everywhere / The ceremony of innocence is drowned.'

The Zen response is to return to the mind. Disruptive behaviours will have originated from diseased thinking, an agent of toxic ideas that may translate into terrifying actions. The enemy in thus located in the nature of mind itself and the solution is to cease thinking altogether.

In psychoanalysis we have seen how Winnicott follows a similar path as he finds in the verbal world and socialization the seeds of mental contamination. Just as the Zen monks, or master and pupil, retreat into an existence that is separated from the world, he and his patient retreat into their own order.

But what about the rest of mankind? If this is a solution for some, is it a cure for all? Or is it a path that only a few can accomplish, leaving the rest of humanity out in the cold to suffer those fates determined by corruption and violence?

From the few we turn to the many, and if we follow a psycho-analytical perspective we move from the individual self, or the intimate analytical couple, to the group. If the Confucian mandates fail to fully effect a social self, if Daoist and Zen retreats fail to remedy such failure, then a psychology must evolve to address the dynamic life of the large group.

Interestingly, Freud himself turned towards a psychology of groups, driven by the shattering lessons of the first world war that ended the Enlightenment-based psychology in the West and forced all but the hermetic to face the reality of group life.

Earlier in his thinking, Freud proposes that it is the sheer power and irreversible effect of the symbolic father that divides the child from omnipotent relationship to the mother and compels the self to accept the laws of socialization. Up to a point this is true. But what Freud tellingly fails to follow up explicitly – although in my view it is implicit in *Group Psychology and the Analysis of the Ego* (1921) – is that it is not the introduction of the name of the father that ultimately dissolves this complex, but the relentlessly evolving effect of group life.

Indeed, ironically enough, the Oedipal conflict is the first group conflict, the first situation that demonstrates how painful it is to be governed by a group psychology uninterested in the self's omnipotent wishes, indifferent to its nuclear origin and unmoved by the name of any father. While the father plays a crucial role in the child's mental life, his destruction by the group – and the structuralization of this fact – is important for any modern self's capacity to live within the real.

If the law is the putative representation of the Oedipal father's effort to govern the group, disobedience, breakdown and lawlessness are vivid evidence of the limits of the paternal order. Although some genocides are orchestrated by a sociopathic father – Hitler, Pol Pot, Mugabe – others, such as the American slaughter of the Vietnamese, are democratically sanctioned group decisions. Indeed, fearing the power of the group, some rulers will impose military rule in an attempt to prevent it from achieving its logic.

Wilfred Bion began his career in psychoanalytic writing by studying groups. His view was that they tend to be governed by psychotic defences.[10] Participation in a Bion group[11] is psycho-analytically efficacious because it promotes an understanding of the primitive parts of the self, driven by envy, hate and revenge and fractured by splitting and projective identification. It is as if the Oedipal self is blinded, not by sightlessness, but by a hatred that turns any victim into an object to be eliminated.

In the psychoanalytic schema, where do we place the group, its psychology, and its impact on the self? Where do we put group process governed not by the hieratic thought system of the paternal order, but by a horizontal thought system driven by powerful affects? How do we honour this dark dimension of our being which, though destructive, is nonetheless a crucial part of human experience?

This topic may seem far removed from the focus of this text. But in reading Lao Tzu, Confucius, Mencius, Mo Tzu and Zhuangzi, and taking into account the matriculation of Zen into Eastern thought, we may pause to consider whether these sages had an awareness of the psychology of the large group. China, always the most heavily populated region of its time, sought an integrated population, one that allowed room for the deep privacy of the inner self (Daoism and Buddhism) as well as a collective responsibility for the social self (Confucianism).

While the Western world flounders in the identity crisis of globalization, in which the aesthetics of individual choice are increasingly subordinated to the commercialism of global corporations, the history of the Eastern world, though certainly not without its difficulties, seems to have paved a way for the individual and the collective to live within a form of dynamic realism.

Somewhere between the almost inaccessible realm of Zen privacy and the personal formality of the neo-Confucian self, the Eastern social matrix has been quietly constructing a new cultural space that integrates the private and the social self. Although such a cultural space is hardly represented either in their religious and ethical texts, or in the novel, poetry or essay, it may be that this evolving matrix respects the necessity of invisible work.

Why give away a perfectly good secret?

Chapter 9

Rifts in Civilization

We often consider death to be the ultimate social taboo, but in fact we seem to have little trouble thinking or writing about it. We claim it is the hardest aspect of our lives, to live in the shadow of death. But is it? Is there not a much more powerful aversion to thinking about that *other* part of our lives: the large groups that have such sway over our existence?

In the previous chapter I maintained that it is the group that breaks up the Oedipal configuration, and that the complexity of the mind (the infinite group of ideas that move through consciousness) dissolves the sense we have of a unity or a coherence to our being. Elsewhere I had written that, even when overwhelmed by the density of the mind's thoughts, the *I* that is embedded in this complexity is a singular thread of being. I then argued that we have a 'sense of self' – the sense deriving from this thread – and that in fact the self *is* that transcendent being derived from continuous sensings given off by the participant 'I'. But that transcendence is predicated, I now think, on negatively hallucinating the real of the group.

Although many Western writers envisioned the construction of the good- enough state (Plato in 'The Republic', Aristotle in 'The Laws', Augustine in 'The City of God', and so on), Confucius and the neo-Confucians understood that for any mass psychology to be developed it had to meticulously interweave individual life into the group and, in turn, to transform group life into an extension of individual ideals. This took thousands of years, thousands of commentaries, thousands of attempts, but what is crucial here is not the outcome, per se, but the continuous effort to achieve it.

It is easy enough to dismiss Maoism as the inevitable result of such an endeavour, and we have little difficulty in describing the ways in which he failed to fulfil his destiny. But part of our refusal of Mao is the repugnance we face when we are compelled to think of those who propose ways of organizing groups as large as a nation. And lest we think that democracy provides a simple solution, we should be sobered by the fact that today's vast groups, composed through international capital under the name of globalization, are not held to account by democracy. Indeed, the increasing hatred of decades of the so-called 'do-nothing' Congress of the United States reveals the unconscious frustration of mass psychology with the impotence of the democratic process.

To think about the large group, then, is to think of an entity whose underlying psychotic nature can at best be held in check by means of a multitude of placating pleasures. The narratives we prefer are those of the evolution of ethnic groups and then of nations, the history of ideas, of commerce and trade, of monarchs and rulers, of religious figures and paragons of virtue, of scientific invention and artistic achievements. We avoid the *other* history of our world.

For this other history is a record of omnipresent destructiveness, of continual genocide by one group against another. It is the dark story of human hate. Barely glimpsed in books and often left untold by those whose ancestors perpetrated persecution and genocide, for those of us who are alive to face this fact it is overwhelmingly disturbing.

Winnicott wrote that we need to live within the illusion of safety. As parents, we bring our children up to believe they are safe even as we present the perils of life in fairy-tale form. These tales are accounts of the murderous dimension that will come to consciousness later, when parents must tell their children the truth that the world is not so safe after all. Prepubescent African-American children learn from their mothers that, come adolescence, it will not be safe to walk the streets. A frightening number will be dead before the age of 30. Their illusion of safety is punctured, just as it is in Gaza, or in neighbouring Israeli villages, or in any community that finds itself the victim of group violence. But people still live with the hope that some day the violence will end, that peace will be restored and that populations will live in harmony.

There is some evidence to support a notion of progress towards civility around the world – we can point to many examples, from Northern Ireland to South Africa. But even as particular communities may recover to some extent from their group madness, it is a disturbing fact of the human collective unconscious that psychic and environmental factors will form a murderous social matrix. No community or society is truly free from this potential destructiveness.

Noting the position of the group analyst who finds himself the object of violent projective identifications, Bion writes 'I believe ability to shake oneself out of the numbing feeling of reality that is a concomitant of this state [of paralysis] is the prime requisite of the analyst in the group.'[1] In like manner, the task of the contemporary psychoanalytical citizen, if I may put it this way, is to shake the self out of the paralyzing state endemic to thinking about the mentality of the group.

It is not simply the case that we are reluctant to think about mass psychology; it is the object of a repression that, in the extreme, constitutes negative hallucination. When thoughts about the reality of the group are repressed they return in derivative form, such as concern about climate change, the spillage of oil or economic recession. Since each of these thoughts is of course legitimate in itself, it authorizes individuals and groups to express a displaced worry about a more disturbing reality: that as a group we humans are in thrall to the death drive. Identity politics – from 'Friends of the Earth' to 'Save the Whales' to 'No more Drilling' – serve as symbolic actions against the repressed, but they are useless in terms of confronting this unconscious destructiveness.

When elements of mass psychology are not merely repressed but negatively hallucinated, then instead of derivatives emanating from such action there is the existence of a 'nothing'. But a 'nothing' that is now a thing; the active presence of a dead zone of the mind. This means that the self or the group is unable to grapple with the worry because the mind has eliminated its capacity to think the thought. Negative hallucination is not simply not seeing something, it rids the mind of the perceptive apparatus that does the seeing. Unlike repression, this form of defence therefore has a degrading effect on the intellectual and sentient capacities of the mind to engage in thinking thoughts that could be vital to the survival of the species. In short, repeated use of negative hallucination produces a psychotic mind unable to perceive, much less deal with, reality.

But what is the alternative?

Confronted by a dire situation – a powerful, hostile North Korea, for example, glaring with psychotic eyes upon South Korea – what can people do? Why shouldn't South Koreans repress this reality? Such repression might even give rise to enjoyable derivatives – films of the walking dead, maybe, or aliens from outer space. Perhaps negative hallucination could empty the mind of the danger of living in the shadow of a psychotic neighbour. Maybe cultural exchanges of music or literature might transform the psychotic other into something more human? After all, we have seen transformation of this kind before.

Imbricated in Confucian and neo-Confucian ethics is a profound understanding of the danger of the group. I believe that the relative marginalization of a psychology of the individual, or attention to the idiom of the self, took place not because of any intolerance for the right of self-development (although it might seem this way) but because mankind made Confucius anxious. He saw in groups something that worried him deeply, and many of his sayings are directly addressed to leaders of his country. He saw that groups, if not formed according to a powerful collective ethic, could be driven by corruption and destructive forces.

Confucius fought form with form. The individual was only ever to be judged by his actions in relation to others, his function in society. His re-formation of the self therefore served the fundamental purpose of re-forming the group.

What if psychoanalysis – the quintessential psychology of and for the self – were to re-frame itself around the group rather than the individual? What if it were to begin with the group and its psychology and then proceed to integrate the reality of the self?

As discussed, Freud hints at this in *Group Psychology and the Analysis of the Ego*. 'We must conclude that the psychology of groups is the oldest human psychology ... what we have isolated as individual psychology, by neglecting all traces of the group, has only since come into prominence out of the old group psychology, by a gradual process which may still, perhaps, be described as incomplete'. But then he immediately back-tracks: 'Further reflection will show us in what respect this statement requires correction' and he argues that individual psychology must be as old as group psychology.[2] He claims that the father of the primal horde was actually free although the horde was bound together. The murderous drive within the group, argues Freud, was evoked by the power of this father whom the horde intended to kill.

Looking back now, it is easy enough to understand Freud's wish. *If only* group life was collective in relation to its patricidal drive then any group was inevitably and ironically bound by the power of the father. Even though the First World War had provided Freud with more than enough proof that the group not only usurps the power of any strong leader but could ultimately be indifferent to an individual 'father' or the name of the father, Freud held on to the safety offered by the paternal order.

Bion disagrees with Freud's theory. He argues that we cannot separate the individual from the group because each person is a member of a group whether he knows it or not. In *Experiences in Groups* Bion explores the common means utilized by individuals to deal with the anxieties endemic to group life. They may try to flee from the group or fight it. They may form pairs and hope that dyadic alternatives will deter the effect of the group. They may turn to an individual member for leadership and become dependent on the hope that this person can guide them through the group experience. If they have a task – if they are a 'work group' – they can, according to Bion, come together and organize selves to become group members in a way that is not harrowing but pleasurable and hopeful. Without a clear task, however, a group will deteriorate into a regressive position governed by paranoid states of mind and primitive defences.

Each group has its own mentality. Bion writes: 'I shall postulate a group mentality as the pool to which the anonymous contributions are made, and through which the impulses and desires implicit in these contributions are gratified.'[3] Any group mentality would by definition 'be opposed to the avowed aims of the individual members of the group'[4] because it is governed by unconscious processes that are not in the control of individuals or indeed of the group itself.

Bion views this conflict as not unfortunate but vital. 'I consider that group mental life is essential to the full life of the individual'[5] he writes, suggesting that any self's frustration with a group is probably due to the fact that a self's idiosyncratic need can never be satisfied individually within the group if it does not accord with the group's psychology. Bion then sets out 'to look for the causes of the group's failure to afford the individual a full life.'[6]

The power of a group to fulfil the needs of the individual member is foreclosed by the group mentality, which Bion now terms 'the culture of the group.' 'The group can be regarded', he concludes, 'as an interplay between individual needs, group mentality, and culture.'[7] Group mentality is 'the unanimous expression of the will of the group', contributed to by the individual in ways not perceptible to him. And if the group mind perceives a member as thinking or behaving 'in a manner at variance with basic assumptions'[8] it may isolate or attack that individual.

We may like to think of ourselves as autonomous, but in reality we cannot but exist as part of a group, serving a function within it. Whether we know it or not, whether we like it or not, and whether we retreat from it or not, we are group animals. Being a member of a group 'gives rise to feelings in the individual that he can never catch up with a course of events to which he is always, at any given moment, already committed.'

Bion continues: 'There is a matrix of thought which lies within the confines of the basic group, but not within the confines of the individual'[9] but as the group 'has not a conscious',[10] the task of thinking about the group will always lie with the individual.

Lacan finds in the discrepancy between the image we have of ourselves ('the imaginary order') and the way we speak of ourselves ('the symbolic order') a rift *(béance)* that sustains alienation in the human being throughout the life span. Bion finds another gap: 'The individual is a group animal at war, not simply with the group, but with himself for being a group animal and with those aspects of his personality that constitute his "groupishness."'[11]

Imagine for a moment that Oriental thought has taken as one of its tasks psychological remedy for the self-in-the-group. Bion writes that 'no individual, however isolated in time and space, can be regarded as outside a group or lacking in active manifestations of group psychology'.[12] I am fairly sure that he read Confucius and I believe that it is his branch of psychoanalysis that offers a bridge to the aspect of the Eastern mind which, starting with the writings of Confucius and the neo-Confucians, has devoted centuries to the problematic of our being a group animal.

As our existence depends on recognition of this reality, the project that is Eastern thought must play a part in our effort to understand human life, just as the project that is psychoanalysis is vital to the quest to understand the internal world of the psyche. Can these two differing approaches to the study of mankind come together in a modern psychoanalysis? If psychoanalysis is not to be regarded in the East simply as a touristic object, what might it have to offer Oriental life and thought ? Whatever that might be, it can arise only out of an integrative collaboration of psychoanalysis with the Eastern project.

In his highly illuminating introduction to the poetry of Wang Wei, David Hinton claims that the 'wilderness cosmology'[13] that underlies all poetic thinking in China, is 'deeply ecological' because it integrates the human and the natural world in an empirical and a spiritual way, to the point where the distinction between human and nature becomes superfluous. He argues that this vision is 'profoundly feminist' and organized around a 'primal cosmology', around a 'generative force' that he maintains can be traced by Palaeolithic practices and belief in a 'Great Mother.' At this point Hinton makes an eloquent plea for the crucial relevance of the ancient Chinese way of thinking:

> In this Western age, vast environmental destruction has grown out of people's assumptions that they are spirits residing only temporarily here in a mere physical world, that the physical world was created expressly for their use and benefit. This makes the Taoist/Ch'an worldview and its expression in poetry such as Wang Wei's increasingly urgent as an alternative vision in which humankind belongs wholly to the physical realm of natural processes.[14]

Might Hinton have happened upon another Chinese preconception? An awareness, originating thousands of years ago, that unless human nature recognizes its place *in* the natural world – not over it, but in it – then human nature will destroy the earth? Hinton is asking that the Western mind turn to the East, but also that the modern East return to its poets, who unconsciously envisioned a danger to the world, one now threatened by economic greed and human contempt for nature.

Chapter 10

Lost in Thought

We are now confronted with the task of imagining how the Daoist, Confucian, Zen Buddhist and psychoanalytic perspectives could combine to form a project for the psychological understanding of the human animal, in individual and group life.

In another work[1] I described Freud's invention of the psychoanalytical method as 'the Freudian Moment'. I was referring to a specific point in time that arrived out of a collective wish within the species that our dreams might be reported to an other, with whom we could understand them through the disseminating and revelatory logic of free association. Since the history of both Western and Eastern literature reveals many occasions when dreamers told their dreams to others, we may say that over many centuries the human race had a preconception of psychoanalysis. That preconception was realized when Freud established the psychoanalytic setting, sitting behind patients reclined on a couch asking them to associate to their dreams. His act conceptualized a new step in human relations.

For centuries the Occidental world has been intrigued by Oriental thought. In my generation writers, poets, philosophers and many others travelled to the East and returned with libraries and with personal experiences of the psychologies of the Orient. The preceding chapters offer a sample of what one Western psychoanalyst finds in Oriental thought. But can we discover any points of convergence that might permit the Freudian project to meet with the triadic domains of Daoism, Confucianism and

Zen Buddhism? In what ways might the Oriental mind develop the Freudian project? Indeed, how might it extend it and in turn be propelled by it into a conjoint project whose time may have come?

Each person is a private culture of the self,[2] derived in part from inherited disposition and then impressed by the innumerable maternal axioms that contribute to what is known but not thought. This privately formed self then becomes part of the wider culture, first through the negotiated axioms of the parental couple, then a particular family that has codified in its assumptions its ancestral inheritances, then the rules of society-at-large. And all of these factors are also subject to change due to the aleatory impact of the real.

Psychoanalytical theories – of the mother-infant relation, the Oedipal complex, latency, adolescence, and so forth – may vary from one part of the world to another, but the *practice* of psychoanalysis is possible in any culture. All it requires is that analyst and analysand commit themselves to a sequence of meetings, usually regularly and frequently over several years, and two distinct phenomena will be revealed.

Through ordinary talk about the self's life, hidden lines of thought will be revealed through the 'implicate logic'[3] of the unconscious links between seemingly disconnected units of discourse. Whether fluent or hesitant, whether expressed in English, Chinese or Urdu, the unconscious speaks in the spaces-in-between. Every discourse has this 'in-between' logic, the unsaid that can often only be heard afterwards, in the intellectual *après-coup* of the Gestalt, when there suddenly arises in the analyst's mind a pattern of thought revealed through the sequence of the spoken. The task of the analyst is to help the analysand listen to the voice of his own unconscious and to learn from it and thus to benefit from transformative insight.

The second distinct phenomenon is that the analysand will form a relationship with his analyst. In the field of the transference the patient will exhibit patterns of behaviour, both verbal and non-verbal, which indicate unconscious axioms that govern his assumptions about being and relating. At the beginning of an analysis these will be conveyed to the analyst as impressions – something about the manner in which the patient speaks, or the way he seems to protect himself, or the assumptions that lie behind a comment or a question. Over time these impressions build up a picture within the analyst's mind of what is distinctive about the patient.

In the assembly of free associations and character articulations the psychoanalyst will work within the parameters of his or her own culture. The wisdom of psychoanalysis lies not in its diverse theories of mind or of psychic development, but in the *process* that it provides.

Psychoanalytical sessions are meditative. Although of course such reverie may be disrupted by the violence of transference and the urgent demands of countertransference for translation, thought and speech, for most of the time the psychoanalyst will be genuinely lost in thought, seemingly mindless.

To be lost in this way is a special form of losing oneself. In what thought? In whose thought? It would be inaccurate to say that the analyst is lost solely in his own thoughts, although this must be true in a narrow sense. He is also lost in the thoughts both spoken and enacted by his analysand. Further, both are lost in the thoughts of previous sessions, in the histories and the ancestries of both personalities and in unconscious transgenerational communications, as well as the cultural thoughts of their social histories.

And what do we mean by 'thought'?

We do not refer simply to consciousness, although of course conscious thinking is part of the world of thought. We are also lost in the unconsciously determined syntax of any participant's word structure, which guides us according to its own thought system. Or, in the case of the fundamentally a-syntactical, non pronominal, tenseless world of classical Chinese, the listener's unconscious is activated by the presentation of an experience in itself.

And then there are the thoughts expressed by the music of the voice, a language every bit as complex in its own ways as the rules of grammar. We must include also the form of thought conveyed in illocutionary action,[4] speech as action-thinking. And of course there are the thoughts expressed by the body,[5] in and through its own terms, those expressed through relationship via transferences and countertransferences ... and so on.

In addition there are the silences between articulations, the liminal states of 'non-being' that precede and follow 'being', punctuating consciousness with present absence.

In order to be truly lost in thought, we as conscious selves must be lost within the structure of the mind as a process; lost not in the contents of thought but in the endopsychic matrix that is mind itself. Being lost in the mind means riding the stream of consciousness as images, fragments of conversation, mnemic invisibles, sexual and aggressive derivatives, and unconsciously determined attractions move us through our life time.

Riding this stream is the journey of ordinary psychoanalysis. It is an experience that the psychoanalyst assumes every time he or she 'sees' a patient – although 'seeing' is hardly representative of what is taking place.

To be sure, there are some clinicians who for personal or cultural reasons are unable to work in this way. There are schools of psychoanalytic thought that advocate a high degree of verbal participation on the part of the analyst. One need not be a neuro-scientist to know that this will activate a very different part of the brain and will produce a self-state (in both participants) very different from the one I have described above. It would never occur to such clinicians to term this interactive dialogue a meditative act, unless that word were to lose any semblance of its historic meaning.

My assumption, however, is that part of the appeal of classi-cally derived psychoanalysis to the Oriental mind is that it constitutes a form of meditative praxis. As I have indicated, it shares many features with Daoist and Buddhist theories of mental practice, especially in appreciation of the road to internal depth.

It does of course differ from these praxes in that, even as both analytic participants are inside a form of meditative state, one of them is talking. Aimlessly. Thoughtlessly. As in a dream.

But talking. And in doing so the analysand *unknowingly* speaks unconscious ideas which are deposited into what Freud termed the great 'storehouse of ideas.' From this depth psychology we learn the psychic truth of the individual self. From this praxis of empty- mindedness and thoughtless speech arrives a stunningly articulate private discourse, spoken through the gaps between units of the enunciated. The act of free association.

In the contemporary Occidental world analysts struggle to help analysands understand that by being relatively quiet, by not engaging in the verbally interactive, by handing themselves over to the process of free association, in time – and with patience – they will hear from themselves, from their parents, from their ancestors, and from their culture. It seems that psychoanalysis can only be enriched by that natural form of inner listening traditionally utilized by the Oriental mind; the power of silence to evoke the movement of the eidetic.

It is a lack of appreciation of this latter expression, the utterances of one's culture, that is perhaps the most serious defect in Western psychoanalysis. And we do well to look to the Oriental mind for an understanding of cultural forms that guide our thought patterns, our self-presentation and self-representation. The Daoist, Confucian and Zen Buddhist assumptions about the virtue of giving oneself over to The Way, about living as a being while accepting the presence of non-being, about mistrusting speech, are reflected in the setting of psychoanalysis and in the theory and practice of analysts such as Winnicott and Khan, as they relinquish speech, listen to the silence and find in being the core of life's meaning.

The classical Freudian theory of free association might seem very far away from the Eastern mind's mistrust of wording the self. But in fact this is not so. The theory of free association states that the unconscious speaks, not in the worded but in the spaces between units of utterance, through the unfolding of a sequence of ideas. It is in this respect, in the awareness of the voice of the absent, that Freud's theory finds a remarkable link to the Eastern view of meaning within silence.[6]

Classical Chinese language can, however, add a new dimension to Freudian free association. Where Freud waited for the emergence of a pattern in the sequence of the seemingly disparate ideas presented in the session, the chain of images presented by Chinese amounts to a more existential free associative process, one composed of moving experiences. In that respect, the chain does not serve to connect ideas that might form into a sentence, but almost the opposite: it *juxtaposes* images with such intelligent force that they form a new emotional object. No Chinese wording could ever have a single meaning, it will always elicit many meanings so that speaker and listener share an experience together, even if what it meant and how it meant it remain unfathomable.

So a Sino-Freudian free associative process would have to include in the theory of a logic of sequence a movement of images that culminates in the creation of a further image or pattern, that presents there and then a new emotional reality. Indeed, perhaps too we should include an awareness of the sonic life of voice. Then we may draw upon Ming Dong Gu's observation (based on his reading of Kong Yingda: 574–648 BCE) about music. He writes that the zither was intended in part to create 'a lingering sound ... from the instrument.'[7] He goes on, 'Since it is suggestive of endless resonance, those reverberations may be comparable to the intro-textual relations of and extra-textual responses to a profound writing: the words of a text have come to an end, but the implications do not'.[8]

Ming Dong Gu's observation puts into place something I have known for a long time but have not been able think until now. Although free associations reverberate along lines of meaning, they are also things-in-themselves, presentational objects that ramify through sessions, connecting to one another, and creating a world altogether different from that of the semantic order.

Chapter 11

Group Mind

Herbert Rosenfeld was one of England's most eminent clinical theorists. In his study of the narcissistic personality disorder he happened upon a metaphor that, long after his death, has influenced generations of clinicians around the world. Rosenfeld likened the mind of the narcissist to a mafia gang,[1] ruled by a powerful leader – a Mafia Don – that was a distillation of all the destructive parts of a personality. Manipulative, cynical, guiltless, murderous, it silenced the good parts of a personality through sheer intimidation. It paid off destructive actions through an imposition of group loyalty and fidelity to the dominant part of the personality and created an inner sense of cohesion based on hate.

Rosenfeld's work is the pinnacle of the creative vision offered by 'object relations psychoanalysis'. It shows how in our internal world we exist as a collection of different selves linked to the objects (mental representations of others and aspects of external reality) within our mind. If we are balanced, then destructive representations will be counteracted by the loving, caring, constructive and ethical parts of the personality.

With analysands I sometimes speak of the mind as a 'representative body'. If I am working with Americans I use the Congress as a metaphor; with Europeans and others I use Parliament. The idea is simple enough: our minds may be thought of as objectifying many different self-states, feelings and conditions. If we are psychic democrats then *all ideas*, including destructive ones, will be represented and allowed to pass through the mind, whether they repel and alienate, or inspire and empower us.

Take for example an analysand who claimed to feel only hatred for her husband, producing as evidence a stream of bitter comments. Now and then she would unwittingly make a passing positive observation about his conduct – how he had fixed the car, taken the children to a park, admired her work. These comments were articulations of her loving feelings which were ordinarily suppressed. In pointing this out to her I would use the metaphor of her mind as a Congress, saying that all her ideas were there in her House of Representatives, even though she was generally governed by a very destructive part of that body of thought. I could usually predict an emotionally violent response: she hated the metaphor and found it simplistic and insulting. I could see that her resistance was due to her fury over its metaphoric transformative potential. It was simply not possible for her to deny the metaphor and this *form* of expression – rather than the content – came to play an increasingly influential part in our ability think about her extreme destructiveness.

It is possible that Rosenfeld's vision of the mind as a group may help us with the problem of integrating the individual and the mass. Bion, and other Kleinian theorists, certainly worked on the assumption that individual and group psychology shared the same mental axioms, but it was Rosenfeld who collected this view into a transformational object. That is, once the bits and pieces of individual and group psychology resident in Kleinian thinking were integrated in Rosenfeld's metaphor, a new form of psychoanalysis became possible.

Considering the ways in which psychoanalysis in the West and in the East might be related, I think the metaphor of the mind as a congress of ideas brings the eremitic tradition of Daoism and Buddhism together with the social ethics of Confucius and the neo-Confucians. We would of course need to include in the parliament of the mind a representative space for the 'no idea' or the 'empty space' or the 'unthought'.

We can see in the cultures of China, Korea and Japan thousands of years of effort to integrate the interiority of the individual self with the transparency of the social self. While some of the more ritualistic and formulaic prescriptions of this tradition would appear to be psychologically anti-democratic (for example the public shaming of noxious behaviour or incompatible ideas), still we observe the attempt to construct a mind that can operate in two worlds: the internal world of mental representation and the external world of articulated actions.

Indeed, when comparing Western and Eastern traditions I think we may discover a project, spanning thousands of years, to create a trans-generational group mind. Although sharing many of the elements of the individual mind, a group mind would be composed of those mental structures set into place by a society with the aim of thinking its own group process. I am not referring here to a conscious project but to an unconscious one. I am suggesting that we rethink the work of history (the constructed narratives of our past), regarding it less as a task of recollection and more as an effort to collect.

By collecting stories from our past, the work of the historian is inevitably futuristic in its thinking. This of course is a truism. Sayings such as 'History will judge' or 'those who cannot remember the past are condemned to repeat it' (Santayana) refer to history as a function of the future. The unconscious work of transferring the achievements of one generation to the next, with its effort to understand and expand the human mind, aims to construct a group mind that can think the thoughts demanded by the future. Indeed, the quest to *understand* the mind and the imbricative *development* of the mind in the process are insepa-rable. To think about our mind is to develop psychic life.

Each generation works at a different pace and will contribute to a greater or lesser extent to the development of a trans-gener-ational mind. This is a discontinuous progression, restrained inevitably by the narcissisms of youth, the depressive anxiety of the aging, and regression to primitive mental states occasioned by collective hatred that can lead to war or genocide and, inter-nally, to a loss of mental capacity.

When one generation 'passes the torch' to the next, claiming that now 'the future is up to them', this is akin to a generational abandonment of the collective task. A successful generational transmission would consist of the passing on of a successful idea or social process that could be incorporated into the future mind. So, for example, had Europe and the United States agreed to allow Hans Blix and the U.N. to investigate adequately the possibility that Iraq was stockpiling arms of mass destruction, this would have supported the place in international affairs of a thinking mind, a mind that needs time for proper investigation and assimilation of data, time for reasoned judgement. The impatience to invade regardless of the Blix Commission's requests was a set-back for the phylogenetic need to develop a mind to think the problems of our times. We are, then, unable to pass on to the next generation evidence of the wisdom of the Blix axiom. However, the debate, especially in the United Kingdom, between those who backed the Blix Commission and those who opposed it did at least reveal how a large group could attempt to think about something as complex as the situation in Iraq.

Mao Zedong is clearly a seminal figure in the trans-generational development of mind, as many of his sayings are clearly derived from a Confucian insistence upon the collective imperative of self-scrutiny and requisite patience over attaining ideals. Westerners often complain about how hard it can be to get the Chinese to be direct, how circumlocutional they seem in their arguments, but this is simply evidence of a different way of thinking. The Chinese expect to be able to think without being rushed into action. In 'On Coalition Government' (April 24,1945) in the *Selected Works* Vol. 111, pp. 316–17 Mao wrote:

> To check up regularly on our work and in the process develop a democratic style of work, to fear neither criticism nor self-criticism and to apply such good popular Chinese maxims as 'Say all you know and say it without reserve', 'Blame not the speaker but be warned by his words' and 'Correct mistakes if you have committed them and guard against them if you have not' – this is the only effective way to prevent all kinds of political dust and germs from contaminating the minds of our comrades and the body of our Party.[2]

The Chinese mind certainly demonstrates the way in which mental structures can be transmitted from one generation to another, from century to century, so that over thousands of years inherited mental axioms eventually constitute collective unconscious forms for being and relating. By invoking Confucius, Mao connects his own project – that of forming a collective mind – with China's greatest social thinker, who had the same project in mind. As we have seen, the trans-generational forms in the East that derive from The Way, value action as thought, ways of being are cherished forms of articulation, and the non-verbal has presentational integrity.

How does one marry the Eastern penchant for the idiompotential of form with the Western interest in the meaning of the spoken word?

I believe this becomes possible when we can see in both traditions these two vital elements of mental life. The East has been concerned with the self as a form, informed, and in-form with the social order; the West has focused on verbal representation as the means of conveying the unique thoughts of a self. However, the life of the mind resides both in the form and the content of the mind and Eastern and Western traditions of thought, presentation, representation, and community do in fact have elements in common.

A meeting of these minds will be part of the task of a transgenerational social mind, and it will require an increasingly inclusive psychic democracy. Western and Eastern axioms will both need representation in the mentality that is essential to the future of civilization. This new mentality must find space both for the highly idiomatic individualism valued in the West and for the deep ethic of a self in social formation emphasized in the East. The Western psychoanalytic mentality will need to understand 'mindlessness' in the Zen tradition and its links with Winnicott's 'formlessness'. In turn, Freud's recognition that the mind delivered into speech reveals a pattern of unconscious thought will be of immense value to the East in understanding the silent dignity of individual mentality.

Are we then speaking of a 'world mentality', a mind that can enable the world to think itself?

The history of the concept of mentality recognizes that minds are different; that one person's mentality will differ from another, just as cultures differ in their assumptions, their habits of thought and their customs of behaviour. If it is true that East and West need increased integration of their respective attitudes to mind, self and society, it is also true that individual differences will always exist – between East and West, between the countries in these worlds, between the cities in each country, between neighbourhoods, between members of the family, between the parts of each self.

A trans-generational social mind, then, has the curious task of collecting a vision of a de-centred mind, a mind that could never be individually or even nationally defined, but that can be *positioned* as a potential space for group thinking. Although we know from the seminal works of Levi-Strauss that different cultures reflect variant mental structures, it does not follow that any two cultures involved in 'cultural exchanges' would be unable to adjust their respective ways of thinking. Indeed, Korea and Japan are excellent examples of countries that, although deeply influenced by Chinese thought, came to this with their own distinctive minds.

However one may fault Mao Zedong, it is incontestable that he was one of the figures who tried to integrate Eastern and Western ways of thinking. Bringing Marx and Lenin to Confucius was no easy step and, however clumsily accomplished, his effort is of intellectual interest. In 'On the Correct Handling of Contradictions Among the People' he writes:[3]

> Between the opposites in a contradiction there is at once unity and struggle, and it is this that impels things to move and change. Contradictions exist everywhere, but they differ in accordance with the different nature of different things. In any given phenomenon or thing, the unity of opposites is conditional, temporary, and transitory, and hence relative, whereas the struggle of opposites is absolute.[4]

Rosenfeld, and all those psychoanalysts influenced by object relations theory, would recognize the psychic truth that contradictions in a group process always mirror contradictions resident in any single mind. Any unity of opposites can only ever be both conditional and ephemeral, as 'the struggle of opposites is absolute.'

The conflict between the complexity and subtlety of the individual private self, known but not communicable, and that self's participation in any group process that assumes the evident to be the truth, is one that will continue as long as we live. The dichotomy between East and West in presenting totally different categories of mind may seem absolute, but, in the end, both civilizations have always been faced with the task of developing parts of the human mind that can be contiguous and cooperative while respecting the inevitable differences of cultural mentality and individual idiom.

Chapter 12

Possibilities

If Oriental psychology has evolved a highly attuned and articulated sense of the forms of human life (individual and collective) it has done so, unwittingly perhaps, at the expense of human representation. Society abounds in rituals to live by, in relational engagements, marriage, family life, community affairs, politics, religion. One presents the self in these forms and in so doing will inevitably find idioms of formal being that are valid hybrids of conventional forms. As discussed, *The Book of Rites* is a manual on how to behave, but it must be read along with *The Book of Songs* if one is to appreciate how the Chinese see form – the form of a poem, the form of behaviour – as strikingly similar projects. There is no such sense, or depth of comprehension, of the formal presentation of self in the Occidental world.

But when it comes to the representation of the self's inner life in language, it is as if the Oriental mind finds itself confronted by the unutterable. Speech may be formally evocative, but the content of the spoken struggles to stray thematically from accepted norms cultivated over centuries.

No wonder that Zen offers freedom for so many who have had to bear the weight of mandated habits, even as over the centuries (especially in Japan)[1] it became a function of the state. And it is no surprise that it also flourished in the United States during the mind-demoralizing era of the Vietnam war and the intellectual nausea of a post-war society saturated with self-congratulatory politics.

Now, as East and West make increasing attempts to meet, psychoanalysis, as one of the possible bridges, finds itself in an intriguing place. Prized in the Western world for its emphasis on free speech that reveals repressed thoughts, psychoanalysis has laid great emphasis on speaking the meaning of a self. But where can this tradition fit in an Eastern world that has little apparent interest in words-from-within?

'I do not want to write in chained words. Chained words tell of things in chains',[2] writes the modern Korean poet Chŏng Hyonjuong in 'The Festival of Pain, 1'. In 'The Abyss of Sound' he again speaks for the Eastern mind:

> Sound knows the ear, love-deepened,
> and steals the ear to shape it for itself
> as an ear attached to sound.[3]

In 'The Abyss of Sound' he adds: 'Sound listens to sound's voice' and 'sound longs for sound's ear.'[4] Perhaps the form of one's being conveys itself through the sound of the word, in the way each voice sings its vocabulary, just as the body portrays the self in the figurative actions of the ordinary gestures of everyday life.

Takeo Doi's work on *amae*[5] recognizes a crucial axiom in the Japanese character, although interestingly enough, he does not link the amae-paradigm to the mother-texts of China. Doi's elegant work examines in convincing detail how the Japanese character is formed on an assumption derived from the mother-infant relation: that each of us has a right to be loved by the maternal features resident in the other.

Amae is the presence of 'passive love' and to *ameru* someone is to provide them with an unquestioned but formalized love. It is assumed, in other words, within the Japanese mind that self must provide for other without being asked to do so. In Japanese cultural relations one always offers some form of gift to a guest – a small present, an offer of food – as a formal representation of a relational necessity. Not to do so would be to insult the other.

Japanese analysts, Doi amongst them, have found that this relational axiom has elongated and extenuated the terms of the maternal order in everyday life. Osamu Kitayama[6] and others have commented on how this deep and lasting form of being and relating has deferred – indeed altered – the classical Oedipal conflict that is so much a focus for the Western mind.

During the early 1950s, Takeo Doi spent two periods of time in the United States as a young resident in psychiatry. He was shocked by the American emphasis on individualism, one feature of which he found to be an insensitivity to the dependent needs of the self. It was not until he read Michael Balint's work 'Primary love and psychoanalytic technique'[7] that he found in a Western voice something akin to what the Japanese meant by *amae*. Reflecting on the American tradition of valuing the independent self and shunning the self's dependency needs, Takeo Doi wrote: 'It brought home to me anew the inevitability of cultural conditioning.'[8]

A decade later his younger and brilliant colleague, Osamu Kitayama, studied psychiatry and psychoanalysis in London. Kitayama was an avid student of Western culture and it was not so easy for him to return to his native Japan where he had to relearn many of its traditions and refind its literary foundations.

As in Takeo Doi's *The Anatomy of Dependence*, Kitayama's *Prohibition of Don't Look* puts an emphasis on formal axioms in Japanese behaviour as well as providing a beautiful essay on 'transience'. Kitayama's book has an afterforward by a Indian colleague and friend, Dr. Jhuma Basak, that places his life and work in context.

In the writings of Takeo Doi and Osamu Kitayama I am struck by what is there, but also by what is not there. In their theory of the Japanese mind they place as much emphasis on the not-said as upon the said, but I believe there is an omission of a different order. Neither writer refers to the influence of the Chinese tradition of thought upon the Japanese mind. But as the *unsaid* has this apparent unsaying simply articulated the obvious?

David Pollard, in his introduction to Lu Xun's novella, *The True Story of Ah Q*, provides a hint as to what might deter the Japanese and Koreans from making reference to their Chinese heritage. Lu Xun's searing satire on Chinese society had as his 'target ...', he said, 'no less than the life and soul of the Chinese people.'[9] 'As early as his student days in Japan Lu Xun had concluded that absence of sympathy was one of the weaknesses of the Chinese character,' writes Pollard. In 1925 Lu Xun said that 'the Chinese are a silent people, unaware of each other as individuals, and unaware of themselves.'[10] Pollard concludes that Lu Xun aimed to bring about recognition of the lack of sympathy rather than to evoke it in the reader.

Centuries of Confucian presentations of forms-for-being may indeed have marginalized the maternal order so prescient in Daoist spiritualism and Zen practice and Lu Xun in Japan – living in the world of *ameru*, of a form of maternal love shared between Japanese people – evoked Lu Xun's critique of the Chinese, his own people. It may also help us to understand why the Japanese may not find themselves in sympathy with the very mother texts that have so influenced them, in that the Japanese may have evolved very different relational axioms from these texts than have the Chinese.

Psychoanalytical investigation of mental life is predicated on the idea that mind is composed of mental structures that evolve over time. Looking into our past we can see how these structures are axioms that influence or partly govern our mentality, our sensibility, and our way of relating. Such assumptions are themselves derived from rules of conduct communicated by mothers and fathers who transmit both thought and unthought known assumptions about being and relating that are resident in their own minds and culture.

It is natural, therefore, for any psychoanalytical investigation of the way someone thinks to examine the history of that person's thought, going back to the beginning. What is of interest in the Japanese and Korean cultures are their long histories of determined isolation, although Japan turned to the Western world a century or more before Korea, which had been the Poland of that region; invaded so many times that it has clung fiercely to its own indigenous traditions that cohered the people during long periods of occupation by the other.

These were, ironically, invasions by other countries that shared something of the same foundational ideas: Japan and

Korea had both been influenced by Daoism, Confucianism, and Buddhism. Yet being invaded by a religious-intellectual cousin does not endear that other to one and this may help to explain in part why the Koreans are less than enthusiastic about acknowledging what they have in common, mentally, with the Chinese and the Japanese.

But what if all three regions, in their effort to differentiate themselves from one another and their eagerness to export themselves to the outside world and to import its products, have done so by repressing China on the mind? What if these long standing forms of thought – somewhat incomprehensible to the Western mind – are also objects of intense ambivalence in the Orient? What if China, Korea, and Japan are more than eager to *lose* their mind?

An irony presents itself. What better way to achieve emptiness of mind, a domain of private formless thought, than by means of a collective negative hallucination? By not recognizing what is held in common, a shared mentality is preserved.

That mindless mind, formed over so many centuries no longer needs representation. Indeed intellectuals of China, Korea, Japan and other countries are free to absent themselves from their own history precisely because it sanctions such absence of thought. By seeming to abandon the Chinese roots of their thought these cultures can preserve their preverbal sanctuary undiscovered. It will remain in the collective unconscious to be owned, perhaps, one day in the future. There seems to have been, in fact, a rather 'on again, off again' approach to the mother-texts and their unconscious axioms; centuries of lack of interest in, for example, Confucius have been punctuated by his periodic return to the forefront of their thinking.

If this is so, then this is not a conscious decision but one made or allowed by default as a collective unconscious inclination. If the West is considered to be the culture that displays the assumptions of the verbal self, the East can hide its originating culture in the realm of non-verbal form. This does not mean that such forms are cultivated in private; indeed, new forms of behaviour may be embraced with great enthusiasm. But another irony is not escaped, that this was a collective decision.

By agreeing to the invasion of the 'verbals' the 'formals' had little choice but to appear to consent to the priority of verbal presentation. Even as the West presented its own forms it did so without Eastern knowledge of the value of forms; indeed, they were assumed to be the forms common to the world. Thus they lost their character.

By embracing the West and ignoring Chinese thought the Chinese, Koreans, and Japanese open the door for Western thinkers and psychoanalysts to speak their forms for them. If I am correct in assuming that *this* moment in history is an evolution occurring over millennia, that the East and the West partitioned the mind in two – one content-orientated, the other form-orientated – then this new trade-relation is most interesting. Communications between these civilizations are not only cultural exchanges but evolutionary integrations of the human mind.

In his astute essay 'Psychoanalytic and Buddhist history and theory'[11] Jeffrey Rubin finds two very distinct differences between Buddhist thought and Western thinking. 'Buddha maintains that all conditioned states of mind inevitably lead to suffering' and he adds that 'by becoming attached to what changes humans, according to Buddha, sow the seeds of their own suffering.'[12] The second assumption is that to extricate oneself from suffering and 'imprisonment' one has to 'reach a state of complete awakening or liberation or Nirvana' in which 'the oneness of all life is evident.'[13] In previous chapters I have argued that the praxes of Winnicott and his disciple Masud Khan (and those who followed in their footsteps) detach a self from its ordinary attachments: to materialist assumptions, to socializing orientation, to the familiar and to speech. By focusing on being rather than speaking they have changed Freudian practice and moved it East.

And Rubin's first distinction would find company in the world of Lacanian praxis where it is indeed assumed that the self's attachment to the Imaginary constitutes a perpetual state of alienation that can only be relieved by an abandonment of that devotion through the liberating effect of hearing from the symbolic order. To be sure, Lacanians do not propose an end to suffering through their praxis; indeed, they see suffering as almost equivalent to being human, but I think we can see a departure from Freud in Lacan's thinking that moves towards the East and away from the West. In its emphasis on the sonic effect of a signifier – like the word 'shoe' also meaning 'shoo!' – Lacan's praxis (ironically enough) finds preverbal links within the symbolic order. Merely attending to the sounds of voice is a deeply maternal order action, even as the rationale may be under the auspices of the name of the father.

Although time does not permit the kind of analysis needed to distinguish crucial differences in the heritage of words, it is still important to point out that what is meant by the self in the West and the East are not the same thing. So when in Zen practice, for example – or in Confucian ethics – it is proposed that the self be dissolved so one may gain Nirvana, we would have to take a long time to determine what was meant by self in the first place, before we could know what was being dissolved and what might emerge in its place. In Wordsworth the self is the quiet centre of one's being, informed by being-in-the world: far away indeed from the 'egotistical.'

I think we can see that both Eastern and Western minds already exist side-by-side in Freudian psychoanalysis. The Western aspect of this praxis is evident to the psychoanalytical world, but the Eastern assumptions are not. It is the attempt to make this explicit that has driven the writing of this book.

In 'The transformational object'[14] I argued that Freud's emphasis on the Oedipal Complex and the role of the father in the formation of psychic structure would seem to marginalize the infant-mother relation, both in his theory and in his practice. But I maintained that the construction of the setting – the dreamily free associating analysand, the evenly suspended analyst living in a state of reverie – *acted out* the mother-infant relationship. What Freud could not put into his theory of the self was represented through an enactment which we may now say was a fortunate step indeed as it lead to the genius of the setting, the process, and the core of the relationship which is the heart of psychoanalysis.

Winnicott and Khan fashioned an entire technique based on a situation that Freud had devised, semi-consciously perhaps, as an enactment of the infant-mother relation. They privileged silence over speech, being over doing (including reflecting), and regression to dependence over individuated developmental progression. They provided a setting in which individuals could have a profound experience, a return to the self's origins. Their focus on regression constituted a valuable extreme from which much was learned. But, as I said earlier, they did not *analyse* their analysands' internal worlds. They eschewed free association and therefore, without Freudian analytic technique to complement it, their approach left the analysand with an understanding of the psychoanalytical experience that, though profound, could only ever be partial.[15]

But the nature of their enactment of the silent side of Freudian praxis remained largely unnoticed even though Winnicott discussed the ways the mother-infant relation was enacted in the transference. Khan was quite clear that the fundamental object relation of psychoanalysis was based on the infant-mother relation: '...the clinical analytic situation is essentially modeled on the infant-mother relationship.'[16] Winnicott comes very close to stating that Freud has enacted the infant-mother relation as psychoanalysis: 'Freud takes for granted the early mothering situation and my contention is that *it turned up in his provision of a setting for his work*, almost without his being aware of what he was doing.'[17] Almost? No, indeed it was entirely repressed by Freud and the significance of the infant-mother relation never found a place in Freud's metapsychology. Winnicott and Khan failed to decode adequately Freud's repression even as they added to its significance.

Would this enactment have escaped the Eastern eye over time? I rather doubt it. But it is interesting that this other way of thinking, relating, and developing the self was repressed by Freud in a way consistent with Western repression of Eastern thoughts about being and relating. Still, at the beginning of the 20th century Western civilization realized something that joined West and East, as the maternal and paternal orders were brought together in what I term 'the Freudian moment.'

It would seem that throughout psychoanalytic history Freud's enacted repression of the maternal has evaded consciousness. But now that Eastern and Western psychoanalysis are beginning to talk to one another, it is crucial to acknowledge the marriage between East and West that, however poorly understood, already exists in the very creation of psychoanalysis.

Winnicott's technique takes Freud's repressed enactment and transforms it into a core praxis. The Western self is now to stop talking, to find in silence forms of endopsychic communion; remarkable varieties of communicating with the equally silent m(other). The aim is to stop self representation so that one may return to inner personal reality or the self's being and to establish a continuity of being from which true-self gestures may emerge. Such gestures are not represented mental contents, not enunciations, they are forms of being that are the self. This is analysis aimed at fostering self presentation.

Although Lacan's theory is certainly paternocentric, as he celebrates the name of the father and the symbolic order his technique is closer to Winnicott's way of working than it is to Freud's. In fact classical Lacanians[18] regard it as fundamentally unethical to interpret anything to a patient. The analyst rarely speaks and when he does he 'punctuates' the session by repeating a word the analysand has spoken, one that connects to other signifiers, and this contributes to the very slow unfolding of the analysand's psychic truth. Lacan accepted that there were many features of his practice that were Zen-like.

Although psychoanalysis is not consonant with the Confucian side of the Eastern mind in that it certainly does focus on the individual self, in the work of Klein, Rosenfeld and especially Bion, psychoanalysis is always a form of group process. Confucius' concern with a self that is both part of the group, and an ethical representative of it, is reflected in Kleinian theory which sees the mind as a group of contending forces that could be summarized as good versus evil, with the analyst on the side of eliminating evil in order that good prevail. This battle within the self and within the analysis may be highly verbal, but even so we find echoes of the Eastern mentality: interpretations may be repeated so many times that sentences become more like mantras and wording moves toward a form of chant.

Taken together, the quietist and the activist branches of psychoanalysis – Winnicott, Khan, and Lacan the quietists, with Klein and Rosenfeld the activists – join the pure realms of being with the politics of place. In other words, British psychoanalysts have over the last seventy years brought into the same place of assembly what could become a new form of psychoanalysis, as Eastern in its orientation as it is Western. And unlike the singular vision of Zen or Daoism, psychoanalysis actually builds into its practice the Confucian emphasis on developing a form within which to live as part of the group.

But will Western psychoanalysts understand what they have been doing? Or will its Eastern dimension remain under repression?

If this reality is emotionally realized by those who participate in East–West meetings – those who are interested in psychoanalysis in China and the Far East and those who find the East of interest in the West – then another important feature of psychoanalysis will be conceptualized. Freud's enactment has always been as much an Eastern moment as a Western one. It has remained unrecognized in itself but should be, at least unconsciously, prescient to those who practice in China, Korea, and Japan.

Winnicott's extreme antipathy to representation and his predilection towards presentation should be emotionally familiar to the Eastern mind, as should Khan's poetic form of enunciation, and Lacan's pristine form of listening with its remarkable care over the 'word', the sound of which may prevail over the sense of the phrase.

These analysts, in other words, are formalists. They have found a new form for psychoanalysis based upon the radical form proposed by the Freudian Pair, predicated upon the sequestration of the mother-infant relation accomplished through repression, and developed through the poetics of Winnicott, Khan, Lacan, Bion and others.

We have seen that in one crucial aspect psychoanalysis accepts, facilitates and functions on a poetic level that would be of deep appeal to an Eastern mind that has functioned for thousands of years according to poetic axioms.

Freud would be the last person to claim that 'free associating', an act of expansive self-representation, neatly coheres the self or resolves the problems posed by the enigmatic features of poetic discourse. Indeed, the questions of who is speaking in narrative, and to whom – an issue concerning the transference and counter-transference between writer and reader – would have been appreciated by Freud, who shied away from proposing a theory of a unified self. The classical Chinese language proposes no speaking subject, only images that present themselves to conjure a reality which the self may experience.

I think Freud would have agreed with Maurice Blanchot who merges the seeming mystery of the poetic and the illusory lucidity of prose. In Blanchot's[19] wisdom, both forms of discourse mingle into the mystery of what we are and what we become whenever we present ourselves or represent ourselves.

> The writer belongs to a language that no one speaks, which is addressed to no one, which has no center, and which reveals nothing. He may believe that he affirms himself in this language but what he affirms is altogether deprived of self. To the extent that, being a writer, he does justice to what requires writing, he can never again express himself, any more than he can appeal to you, or even introduce another's speech. Where he is, only being speaks – which means that language doesn't speak anymore, but is. It devotes itself to the pure passivity of being.[20]

In fact, Blanchot's assertion of the solitude of the writer both epitomizes the views of post modernist Western writers and also characterizes two thousand years of Eastern thinking about the impossibility of representation.

Psychoanalysis recognizes through its sheer fecundity of unconscious movement within the analytical experience the absurdity of speaking it; a relational phenomenon in many ways, it is nonetheless a solitary act committed by two people engaged in it together. That which can be communicated and known, and the nothing that cannot, combine to make psychoanalysis a unique venture in self experience that mutates into differing forms of self knowledge.

Chapter 13

Coda

Outside a temple in Kyoto I sat on the long stairs climbing the entrance, listening to the chanting inside. I had a vivid sense that I had been there before; indeed, that I had lived a life here before. It was a classic *déjà vu* experience. What if this experience was an unconscious epiphany that recognized the historical precedents for my emotional experience? What if we all have a sense of having lived a past life somewhere else, as someone else, because we have? What if, in other words, my Western self experienced its Eastern self, once known thousands of years ago?

For the argument proposed here is not that Eastern and Western minds have nothing in common but that they went in different mental directions, both cultivating parts of the human psyche that are intrinsic to mental life. It is not that the Western and Eastern minds cannot comprehend one another's ways of thinking. However it will take time for the Eastern mind to rediscover its Western strands and for the Western mind to rediscover its Eastern forms.

When thinking about my *déjà vu*, I realized I heard Philip Glass and Olivier Messien in the chanting. They had been there well before me. Connecting the Western mind back to its Eastern half.

This essay is an attempt to come to terms with that visit to Japan.

In reading about Oriental cultures before my journey I *developed* certain preconceptions. What I did not then know was that this was a form of re-reading, as the elements of mind developed in the Orient were a part of my own mind and of the minds of people all around the world. To experience the Japanese mind *in vivo*, however, was to realize something that had a profound effect upon me, even though I did not understand it. After my journey, by turning to the foundational texts of the Far Eastern world, I was able to conceptualize this realization.

I found something *present* in the Japanese character that both was and was not *missing* in me. In the unthought known I knew the Japanese articulation of form-as-communication very well: it is the relational world constituted out of the infant-mother *Umwelt*. But in the Western world, the Oedipal complex separates this form of being and relating out from a self, represses it for the most part, and the self is left distanced from the core of its being.

My colleagues and friends in Japan have stated that they do not find it impossible to comprehend and adapt to Western linear thinking, to Western logic, indeed to the Western way of speaking the self. I shall presume that for them, too, it is a matter of 'remembering' a form of thinking, expressing, and relating that is mentally possible.

Is it simply that the Eastern mind has not used the Western idiom so much? To be sure, it has been more difficult for them to return to their own culture and therein to express the Western mind in their own society, but with increased Westernization in the Far East one is seeing, no doubt, an integration of resident but segregated mental possibilities.

A thread through both frames of mind, however, is poetry. Although western poetry is more syntactical and tense filled than Eastern poetry, both traditions rely upon the conjuring of powerful images or emotional experiences that make irrelevant any theme that could be gleaned from them. Indeed, we can see certainly with Ezra Pound, William Carlos Williams and, more latterly, Gary Snyder, Robert Creely and Robert Hass not only an increased interest in Eastern poetry but a movement within their own works toward mental reconciliation between East and West.

How intriguing it is that in poetry, this other discourse so close to the language of the unconscious, the human mind should have retained a common language that might one day form a bridge between two divergent frames of mind.

In 'Kunlun Mountain'[1] (October of 1935) Mao Zedong, a prolific and gifted poet in his own right, accords with the Eastern tradition of poetics and honours the power of a thing in itself: in this case a 'greenblue monster' of a mountain. It has seen many things: changing colours, the comings and goings of men, many snowfalls, and the heat of many seasons. It has seen 'men turn into fish and turtles'.

> Who can judge
> A thousand years of accomplishments or failures?

he writes.

But in a remarkably apt conceit Mao then expresses a wish. He addresses the mountain:

> If I could lean on heaven, grab my sword,
>   And cut you in three parts,
> I would send one to Europe, one to America,
>   and keep one part here
>   in China
> that the world have peace
> and the globe share the same heat and ice.

By wishing to divide the mountain equally amongst these three continents, enabling others to share its universality and transcendent being, Mao foresees the possibility of bringing East to West through the self's wonder over being a part of life itself.

When he was a boy of eight, Mao read the five classics[2] as well as Confucius. Before he was a teenager he began his reading of the great Chinese novels, and when at school in Hunan his reading included Darwin, Adam Smith, John Stuart Mill, Rousseau, Spencer, Montesquieu, Spinoza, Kant and Goethe. He did all of this before he came across Hegel or Marx so by the time he was a young man he had integrated into his remarkable mind not only the classic texts of the East but also those of the West. And of course he read and wrote poetry.

His wish to divide the mountain is a desire to share the qualities held by the poetic imagination as it oversees the universals of human life. Like the mountain, the poetic mind exists for thousands of years. Many people in many lands have grasped the real through the uncanny power of poetic vision. Assembling the people of the world to that vantage point, to see what can be viewed through the lens of poetry, is a very long march indeed.

In some respects, Freud *found* psychoanalysis. It was a monumental moment in the history of human relations, but like Mao's mountain, Freud may well have received a gift from the East of which he was unaware. Now that Western and Eastern psychotherapists and psychoanalysts have begun an earnest dialogue with one another one hopes that the Eastern aspects of psychoanalytical praxis may be appreciated by Western clinicians, lest it remain repressed to the disadvantage of all.

Notes

Intoduction

1 Legalism was one of the main philosophical schools of thought during the Warring States era (475 BCE to 221 BCE) of Chinese history. It argued that human behaviour was too chaotic and people needed to develop laws that would govern their behaviour.

2 See *Hsün Tzu: Basic Writings*, trans. Burton Watson. New York: Columbia University Press, 1996.

3 Jacques Gernet, *A History of Chinese Civilization*. Cambridge: Cambridge University Press, 2008, p. 97.

4 David L. Hall and Roger T. Ames, *Anticipating China: Thinking Through The Narratives of Chinese and Western Cultures*. Albany: State University of New York Press, 1995, p. 54.

5 C. Scott Littleton (ed.), *The Sacred East: Hinduism, Buddhism, Confucianism, Daoism, Shinto*. London: McMillan, 1996, p. 8.

6 Jacques Gernet and Jean-Pierre Vernant, 'Social history and the evolution of ideas in China and Greece from the sixth to the second centuries B.C.' in Jean-Pierre Vernant, *Myth and Society in Ancient Greece*. New York: Zone Books, 1988, pp. 79–100, (p. 84).

7 Born in the 4th century BCE, and key defender of Confucius' views, Mencius believed men were essentially good and proposed self development along lines of the good, in contrast to another neo-Confucian, Xunzi (3rd century BCE) who believed human beings were corrupt and not good. Neo-Confucianism became a centuries-long debate over the forms a society should take in order to mould the human self. Scholars vary considerably over whether to write about Mencius' or Lao Tzu's works as if they were authored by a single individual. Indeed, it is now common practice to refer to 'the Mencius' or 'the Lao Tzu' and other works. This is because almost certainly 'their' works were compiled by many writers over

long periods of time. To simplify matters I will treat these works as if they were authored by the individuals whose name they bear.

8   Gernet and Vernant, 'Social history', p. 85.
9   Ibid., p. 85.
10 Ibid., p. 85.
11 Ibid., p. 86.
12 Ibid., p. 86.
13 Ibid., p. 87.
14 Ibid., p. 89.
15 Ibid., p. 90.
16 Ibid., p. 90.
17 Ibid., p. 94.
18 In their informative and intelligent essay 'Bollywood and the Indian Unconscious' Akhtar and Choksi begin by describing Bollywood films as characteristically driven by 'high affect' (p. 139), with narratives that 'readily lapse into fantasy sequences' and are possessed of 'a hallucinatory and dreamlike quality' (p. 140). At the end of the essay they wonder, 'Could it be that movies in India represent a secular religion for a people who seem to have an intrinsic yearning for worship? Could going to the movies be a form of *darshan* (Hindi word for catching the sight of revered gurus or religions icons)' (pp. 170–1) they conclude? It seems to me that Bollywood *is* the secular extension of the fecund Hindu imagination, its dreamlike cinema startlingly similar to the dreamscape of its gods, demons, and heroes. See *Freud Along the Ganges: Psychoanalytic Reflections on the People and Culture of India,* edited by Salman Akhtar. New York: The Other Press, 2005.
19 To simplify, I will usually refer to these works in their English translations rather than by their Chinese names.
20 The unthought known refers to unconscious knowledge that is derived from implicit rules for being and relating communicated to the self by the mother (and others) during the formative years of infancy. What is known is not thought about but conveyed, usually through behaviours, but also through emotional communication and implicit assumptions lived out by others and by the family. See Christopher Bollas, *The Shadow of the Object: Psychoanalysis of the Unthought Known.* London: Free Association Books, 1987.
21 See Willis Barnstone, 'Introduction' in *The Poems of Mao Zedong.* Berkeley, Los Angeles, London: University of California Press, 1997, p. 3.
22 Gernet, *Chinese Civilization*, p. 34.
23 Quoted by Edward Slingerland in his 'Introduction' to the *Analects.* Indianapolis, Cambridge: Hackett Publishing Company, 2003, p. xxv.

Chapter One

1 See C. G. Jung, 'Forward to the "I Ching"' in 'Psychology and Religion: West and East' in Volume 11 of *The Collected Works of C. J. Jung*. Princeton: Princeton University Press, 1989, pp. 589–608, (p. 591).

2 Accounts of the history of the *I Ching* vary considerably as to, for example, just how many hexagrams were added by Yu. The *I Ching* was not fully standardized until the Zhou Dynasty (1122–256 BCE).

3 R. Wilhelm's translation of the standard text is the one on which most modern versions are based.

4 Li Po, *The Selected Poems of Li Po*, trans. David Hinton. London: Anvil Press Poetry, 2010, p. 110. All citations of Li Po's poetry are from this edition.

5 Hellmut Wilhelm and Richard Wilhelm, *Understanding the I Ching*. Princeton: Princeton University Press, 1995.

6 Ibid., p. 59.

7 Jung, 'Forward to the "I Ching"', p. 592.

8 A remarkable era when, due to technological changes and economic growth, the forces for the centralization of China overcame the power of local small kingdoms through the force of arms and the imposition of rules of law and behaviour.

9 Jacques Gernet writes 'A few figures will suffice to bring home to us the scale of these transfers of population. In 127, 100,000 peasants were settled in Shuo-fang, north-west of the Ordos bend, right in Mongolia; in 102, 180,000 soldier-farmers went off to people the Chiu-ch'uan and Chang-yeh commanderies; and in 120, after big floods in western Shangtung, 700,000 victims of the disaster were transferred to Shensi.' *Chinese Civilization*, p. 121.

10 In *The Selected Poems of Tu Fu*, trans. David Hinton. London: Anvil Press, 1990, p. 31.

11 Ibid., p. 68.

12 Ibid., p. 10.

13 Ibid., p. 31.

14 Ibid., p. 55.

15 Ibid., p. 62.

16 See Lu Xun *The True Story of Ah Q*, trans. Yang Xianyi and Gladys Yang. Hong Kong: The Chinese University Press, 2003.

17 See *The Selected Poems of Li Po*, trans. David Hinton. London: Anvil Press, 1998, p. 110.

18 See Christopher Bollas, 'The destiny drive' in *Forces of Destiny: Psychoanalysis and the Human Idiom*. London: Free Association Books, 1989, pp. 23–49.

Chapter Two

1 David Hinton, 'The Book of Songs' in *Classical Chinese Poetry: An Anthology*, David Hinton (ed.). New York: Farrar, Straus and Giroux, 2008, p. 8.

2 From David L. Hall and Roger T. Ames, *Dao de Jing: Making this Life Signficant*. New York: Random House, 2003, p. 7.

3 *The Book of Songs (Shi Jing)*, trans. Arthur Waley, edited by Joseph Allen. New York: Grove Press, 1996.

4 As Peter H. Lee writes of the Korean hyangga song 'the basis of its prosody is a line consisting of metric segments of three or four syllables … in the ten-line hyangga the ninth line usually begins with an interjection that indicates heightened emotions, a change in tempo and pitch, and presages the poem's conclusion.' Peter H. Lee, *The Columbia Anthology of Traditional Korean Poetry.* New York: Columbia University Press, 2002, p. 4.

5 See Lee, *Anthology of Traditional Korean Poetry*, p. 49.

6 Ibid., p. 69.

7 All the poets cited in these two pages are from Lee's translation.

8 Ibid., p. 108.

9 Ibid., p. 109.

10 Ibid., p. 129.

11 Ibid., p. 135.

12 Ibid., p. 142.

13 Ibid., p. 136.

14 In *The Penguin Book of Japanese Verse: From the Earliest Times to the Present* trans. Geoffrey Bownas and Anthony Thwaite. London: Penguin Classics, 2009, pp. 33–4.

15 See R. H. P. Mason and J. G. Caiger, *A History of Japan*. Tokyo: Tuttle, 1997, p. 83.

16 Bownas and Thwaite, *Penguin Book of Japanese Verse,* p. 51.

17 Ibid., p. 73.

18 *Modern Korean Literature*, Peter H. Lee (ed.). Honolulu: University of Hawai'i Press, 1990.

19 Cecilia Lindquist, *China: Empire of Living Symbols*. Cambraidge, MA: Da Capo Press, 2008.

20 Ibid., p. 144.

21 See *Chinese Poetry: An Anthology of Major Modes and Genres*, ed. and trans. Wai-Lim Yip. Durham, NC and London: Duke University Press, 1997.

22 Wai-Lim Yip, *Chinese Poetry*, p. 15.

23 See 'The Yellow Bicycle' in Robert Hass, *Praise*. New York: The Ecco Press, 1979, p. 8.

24 Wai-Lim Yip, *Chinese Poetry*, p. 79.

25 See Maurice Blanchot 'death as possibility' in (1955) *The Space of Literature*, trans. Ann Smock. Lincoln: University of Nebraska Press,1989, pp. 87–107, (p. 88).

26 See Bonnie S. McDougall and Kam Louie, *The Literature of China in the Twentieth Century*. New York: Columbia University Press, 1997, p. 82.

27 Some will disagree with this and point to Sanskrit writings as the earliest forms of the novel. The *Dasakumaracarita (What Ten Young Men Did)* by Dandin is a 7th-century Indian narrative of the adventures of ten men that demonstrates a high degree of perceptive skill in narrating aspects of Indian culture. The *Kadambari* by Banabhatta, a Sanskrit novel from the 7th century, also follows a narrative prose structure, as does the 12th-century work *Hayy ibn Yaqdha* although that is more a philosophical treatise than it is narrative fiction.

28 See Ming Dong Gu, *Chinese Theories of Fiction: A Non-Western Narrative System*. Albany: State University of New York Press, 2006, p. 97.

Chapter Three

1 The Book of Rites (Li Chi). Edited by James Legge in 1885. New York: Kessinger Publishing, undated, p. 1.

2 Ibid., p. 63.

3 Ibid., p. 75.

4 Ibid., p. 71.

5 Ibid., p. 77.

6 Ibid., p. 89.

7 Ibid., p. 103.

8 Ibid., p. 93.

9 Ibid., p. 64.

10 Ibid., pp. 64–5.

11 All references to the *Analects* are from the Slingerland translation. It is divided into Books and each Book into sections, hence the numbering above: 8.2.

12 See Christopher Bollas, 'Why Oedipus?' in *Being a Character: Psychoanalysis and Self Experience*. London: Routledge, 1993, pp. 218–46.

13 For a discussion of the differing ways in which Confucius uses of the concept of the Good, see Slingerland, *Analects*, p. 238.

14 In *Being a Character* I distinguish between the 'simple experiencing self' and the 'complex self'. The simple self is the figure in the dream, for example, while the complex self would be the dream itself. We oscillate between a position of being lost inside

our experience as a simple self and a position of objective observing and thinking as a complex self. In Bion's terms, the simple self would be the contained; the complex self the container. See *Being A Character*, pp. 15–17.

15 From *The Basic Writings of C.G. Jung* edited by Violet S. de Laszlo, trans. R. F. C. Hull. Princeton: Princeton University Press, 1990, p. 122.

16 See Geza Roheim, (1950) *Psychoanalysis and Anthropology*. New York: IUP, 1969.

17 See Gordon Lawrence (ed.), *Social Dreaming and Work*. London: Karnac, 1998.

Chapter Four

1 The *Tao Teh Ching* or *Tao Te Ching*, or *Daodejung* has almost as many variant spellings as does Lao Tzu: Lao Tse, Lao Tu, Lao-Tzu, Laotze, Lao Zi, and so forth. Indeed, the movement in his name is referred to either as Daoism or Taoism. Unless quoting from another author, I shall follow the spellings above.

2 I can recommend two contemporary versions of the *Dao*. The version edited by Stephen Addiss and Stanley Lombardo (*Tao Te Ching*. Indianapolis/Cambridge: Hackett Publishing Company, 1993) is rightly acclaimed for its almost literal poetic rendering of the *Dao*. For a less sparse and more extenuated version, I recommend the equally highly acclaimed version by Hall and Ames. See *Dao De Jing: Making This Life Significant* edited by David L. Hall and Roger T. Ames, New York: Random House, 2003.

3 See D. W. Winnicott (1965) 'The theory of the parent-infant relationship' in *The Maturational Process and the Facilitating Environment*. London: Hogarth Press, 1972, p. 54.

4 See D. W. Winnicott (1952) 'Anxiety associated with insecurity' in *Through Paediatrics to Psycho-Analysis*. London: Hogarth Press, 1975, p. 99.

5 The work of Alessandra Piontelli addresses the transition from foetus to child in a very astute and creative way. See Alessandra Piontelli *From Fetus to Child: An Observational and Psychoanalytic Study*. London and New York: Routledge, 1992.

6 In England, and Europe, jokes abound about 'nanny England', with its generous welfare system, about the English garden as a realm of nurturance, about the English affection for dogs, and so forth. It is commonplace in England to use for ordinary address terms of endearment such as 'Sweetie', 'Darling', or 'Love'. Historically, the imperialist British brought back to their country social and mental fabrics from the East, and this may have had some influence

on why the English psychoanalysts (unlike others elsewhere) took so naturally to emphasizing the infant-mother relation and the ordinary fact of dependence.

7 See D. W. Winnicott (1962) 'Ego integration in child development' in *Maturational Process*, p. 61.

8 See D. W. Winnicott (1971) *Playing and Reality*. London: Routledge, 2005, p. 74.

9 See D. W. Winnicott, *Human Nature*. London: Free Association Books, 1988, p. 132.

10 See D. W. Winnicott (1960) 'Parent-Infant Relationship' in *The Maturational Process*, p. 140.

11 See D. W. Winnicott, 'Creativity and its origins' in *Playing and Reality*, pp. 87–114.

12 Ibid., p. 97.

13 See Sigmund Freud (1915) 'The Unconscious' in *The Standard Edition of the Complete Psychological Works of Sigmund Freud*, Vol. XIV. London: Hogarth Press, 1995, p. 204.

14 See Christopher Bollas, *The Shadow of the Object*; *The Mystery of Things*. London: Routledge, 1999; and *The Evocative Object World*. London: Routledge, 2009.

15 See Christopher Bollas, 'Psychic genera' in *Being A Character*, pp. 66–100. A psychic genera is formed from the work of the receptive unconscious that, rather like a psychic magnet, draws to it both endogenous and exogenous realities that combine into a new mental structure that then affects the way the individual perceives reality.

16 See Christopher Bollas, 'The transformational object' in *The Shadow of the Object*, pp. 11–29.

17 See D. W. Winnicott, 'Dreaming, fantasying, and living' in *Playing and Reality*, p. 45.

18 In his work with an adolescent, Khan describes in meticulous detail how he felt the different forms of silence expressed by his patient. He writes: 'My role and function during his silences was to provide a sentient, concentrated, alert attention. This attention had to be more than merely listening. It is listening with one's mind and body.' See 'Silence as communication' in Masud Khan, *The Privacy of the Self*. London: Hogarth Press, 1973, pp. 168–80, (p. 174). Although he shied away from such an admission, I suspect that Khan listened in this manner to all his analysands. In this way his technique was analogous to Eastern ways of receiving the other and communicating self to other.

19 See in particular 'A theory for the true self' in *Forces of Destiny*, pp. 7–22.

20 Objects have 'integrity': their own form. This will be discussed at length in the next chapter.

21 See Christopher Bollas, 'What is this thing called self?' in *Cracking Up: The Work of Unconscious Experience*. London: Routledge, 1995, pp. 146–79.

Chapter Five

1   See Christopher Bollas, 'Preoccupation unto death' in *Cracking Up*, pp. 71–102.
2   See Christopher Bollas, *The Freudian Moment*. London: Karnac Books, 2007. Perceptive identification refers to the self's capacity to perceive the integrity of any object. It is to be distinguished from projective identification, which distorts the object through the self's projective actions.
3   See Christopher Bollas, 'A Theory for the true self' in *Forces of Destiny*, pp. 8–12.
4   Gordon W. Allport, *Becoming*. New Haven: Yale Univesity Press, 1955.

Chapter Six

1   All citations are from the Edward Slingerland translation of *The Analects*.
2   Watson, *Hsün Tzu: Basic Writings*.
3   Ibid., p. 89.
4   Ibid., p. 94.
5   Ibid., p. 105.
6   Ibid., p. 100.
7   Ibid., p. 97.
8   See Ming Dong Gu (2006), 'The filial piety complex: variations on the Oedipus theme in Chinese literature and culture' in *The Psychoanalytic Quarterly* 75: 163–95.
9   Citations from Sowŏl's poetry are from David R. McCann (ed.), *The Columbia Anthology of Modern Korean Poetry*. New York: Columbia University Press, 2004, p. 19.
10 Ibid., p. 19.
11 Ibid., p. 21.
12 Winnicott, *Playing and Reality*, p. 101.
13 Ibid., p. 154.
14 See Boye Lafayette De Mente, *The Chinese Mind: Understanding Traditional Chinese Beliefs and Their Influence on Contemporary Culture*. Tokyo: Tuttle, 2009, p. 40.
15 Heinz Hartmann argued that defences can be neutralized thereby losing contact with their original aim; indeed, they may become adaptive, integrative, synthetic, and 'conflict free'. To my way of

thinking, Hartmann was on his way to a theory of ego-as-form (and form maker), an important development in the history of psycho-analysis. However, as so often happens, neither he nor his followers could identify and work with the categorical difference between his theory of the ego and Freud's concept of repression, which were completely different concepts of mental action. See Heinz Hartmann (1939), *Ego Psychology and the Problem of Adaptation*, trans. David Rapaport. New York: International Universities Press, 1958.

16 Hall and Ames, *Dao De Jing*, p. 22.
17 Ibid., p. 22.
18 For a discussion of the fourth object and fourth object relations please see Christopher Bollas, 'The fourth object and beyond' in *The Evocative Object World*, pp. 95–113.

Chapter Seven

1 All quotes from the work of Zhuangzi are from the Burton Watson edition, *Zhuangzi: Basic Writings*. New York: Columbia University Press, 2003.
2 Ibid., p. 27.
3 Ibid., p. 33.
4 Ibid., p. 33.
5 Ibid., p. 34.
6 Ibid., p. 35.
7 Ibid., p. 38.
8 Ibid., p. 38.
9 Ibid., p. 41.
10 Ibid., p. 42.
11 Ibid., p. 43.
12 Ibid., p. 114.
13 Ibid., p. 114.
14 Clare Winnicott said that 'Donald' would try to read philosophy but after two pages would get restless and impatient and throw the book down or across the room. (Personal communication).
15 To read Winnicott's refutation of free association, see D. W. Winnicott (1971) 'Playing: creative activity and the search for the self' in *Playing And Reality*. London: Penguin, 1974, pp. 62–75.
16 Masud Khan claimed that a Winnicottian analysis would destroy any analysand but that one had to put up with such a destruction in order that the core self could emerge as a true self. (personal communication).
17 See 'parent-infant relationship' in *The Maturational Processes*, p. 46.
18 From 'The aims of psychoanalytical treatment' (1962) in *The Maturational Processes*, pp. 166–70, (p. 167).

19 Anxious, perhaps, about disapproval from his peers, Khan rarely alluded to his style of working and in fact misrepresented his idiom by focusing on what he presented as exceptional moments in an otherwise classical context. In fact, no such classical context existed in his practice. See 'Vicissitudes of being, knowing, and experiencing in the therapeutic situation' in *The Privacy of the Self*, pp. 203–18. Reading between the lines, one can sense his emphasis on the need to allow the patient to establish his own 'being' through 'experiencing' in the presence of a sentiently silent analyst. 'Knowing' emerges out of this and, although Khan states that such knowing must be framed by analytical interpretation, he emphasizes the role of 'uninterpretation' and adds, 'it is essentially *not-interpreting* that is the analyst's contribution. To the question of *what* is not being interpreted, the answer is ambiguous.' (p. 205) It is this ambiguity that characterizes Khan's clinical style, and it is close to the Eastern tradition of indirect and allusive communicating, and a mind that thrives on the freedom of ambiguity.

20 There are two different forms of Zen in Japan: *Rinzai Zen* and *Soto Zen*. The first is based on a teacher/student relationship in which the master gives the student a *koan* (riddle) to figure out and answer. Enlightenment is sudden: it comes in a flash. The second is based on meditation, *zazen*, by means of which enlightenment is gradual and imbricative. See Dr. Ornan Rotem 'Buddhism' in C. Scott Littleton, *The Sacred East*, pp. 54–91. Khan's praxis can be seen as combining both forms of Zen as he sustained long periods of meditative 'going on being' broken now and then by brief, stunning, poetic statements of a highly enigmatic type.

21 See Christopher Bollas, 'Masud Khan – portrait of an extraordinary psychoanalytic personality' in *The Guardian*, June 26 1989, p. 39.

22 See Michael Balint, *The Basic Fault: Therapeutic Aspects of Regression*. London: Tavistock, 1968.

23 In D. W. Winnicott, *Playing and Reality*, p. 74

24 Ibid., p. 75.

25 See 'the parent-infant relationship' in *The Maturational Processes*, pp. 52–4.

26 In Winnicott, *Playing and Reality*, p. 76

27 Ibid., p. 86.

28 Certainly Nina Coltart *did* know of the connections between her way of practice and Daoism and Zen. She practised Zen for decades.

29 See Bollas, 'The transformational object' in *The Shadow of the Object*, pp. 13–29.

Chapter Eight

1 Robert E. Buswell Jr., *Cultivating Original Englightment: Wŏnhyo's Exposition of the Vajrasamadhi-Sutra*, Honolulu: University of Hawai'i Press, 2007.
2 Ibid., p. 63.
3 Winnicott, *Playing and Reality*.
4 Ibid., p. 87.
5 See Chinul, *Tracing Back the Radiance: Chinul's Korean Way of Zen*, Robert E. Buswell Jr. (ed.). Honolulu: University of Hawai'i Press, 1991.
6 Ibid., p. 98.
7 The 'area of formlessness' is discussed in 'Dreaming, fantasying, and living' in *Playing and Reality*, pp. 45–50. Winnicott believes the infant is born in an 'unintegrated' state from which emerges being and the potential for true self living. One of the tasks of analysis is to return the patient to formlessness: 'the experience is one of a non-purposive state, as one might say a sort of ticking over of the unintegrated personality', (p. 74).
8 Chinul, *Korean Way of Zen*, p. 99.
9 Ibid., p. 105.
10 See Wilfred Bion, *Experiences in Groups*. London: Tavistock, 1961.
11 Held every April in Leicester, sponsored by the Tavistock Clinic in London. Also sponsored by the A. K. Rice Institute which holds similar conferences in Philadelphia in July of every year and in other cities in North America.

Chapter Nine

1 See Bion, *Experiences in Groups*, p. 149.
2 See Freud, 'Group Psychology and the Analysis of the Ego' in *Standard Edition* Vol. XVIII, pp. 67–143, (p. 123).
3 Bion, *Experiences in Groups*, p. 50.
4 Ibid.
5 Ibid, p. 54.
6 Ibid, p. 50.
7 Ibid, p. 55.
8 Ibid., p. 65.
9 Ibid., p. 91.
10 Ibid., p. 94.
11 Ibid., p. 131.
12 Ibid., p. 132.

13 See David Hinton, 'Introduction' in Wang Wei, *The Selected Poems of Wang Wei*, trans. David Hinton. London: Anvil Press, 2009, pp. xiii–xxi, (p. xiv).

14 Ibid., p. xv.

Chapter Ten

1 Bollas, *The Freudian Moment*.

2 Christopher Bollas, 'Le langage secret de la mère et de l'enfant' in *Nouvelle Revue de Psychanalyse*, Automne 1976. Paris: Gallimard, 1976.

3 See David Bohm (1980), *Wholeness and the Implicate Order*. London and New York: Ark, 1988.

4 See John L. Austin, *How To Do Things With Words*. Oxford: Oxford University Press, 1975.

5 See William F. Cornell, *Explorations in Transactional Analysis: The Meech Lake Papers*. International Transactional Analysis Association, 2008.

6 For a detailed description of the free associative process, including clinical case examples of how all analysands think unconsciously please see Christopher Bollas, *The Infinite Question*. London: Routledge, 2009.

7 See Ming Dong Gu, *Chinese Theories of Reading and Writing: A Route to Hermeneutics and Open Poetics*. Albany: State University of New York Press, 2005, p. 50.

8 Ibid., p. 53.

Chapter Eleven

1 See Rosenfeld's write-up of the case of 'Simon' in 'Destructive narcissism and the death instinct' in *Impasse and Interpretation*. London: Tavistock, 1987, pp. 105–32.

2 In *Quotations From Chairman Mao Tse-Tung* edited by Lin Piao. People's Republic of China, 1966, p. 260.

3 February 27, 1957, 1st pocket edition, p.18. Peking: Foreign Language Press, 1957.

4 From *Quotations From Chairman Mao Tse-Tung*, p. 214.

Chapter Twelve

1 During the Nara period Buddhism was very powerful and dominated the government. As power shifted to the new capital, Kyoto, it was carefully controlled and a new form emerged – Tendai Buddhism – inspired by the great religious figure Saicho (767–822). He

advocated a Buddhism that would help in government adminis-
tration (see Mason and Craiger, *A History of Japan*, p. 99), and at
this point Confucianism and Buddhism therefore converge in the
shared task of weaving the individual into the collective.

2 In Lee, *Modern Korean Literature*, p. 306.

3 Ibid., p. 302.

4 Ibid., p. 303.

5 Takeo Doi, *The Anatomy of Dependence: The Key Analysis of
Japanese Behavior*, trans. John Bester (2nd edn). Tokyo: Kodansha
International, 1981.

6 See Osamu Kitayama, *Prohibition of Don't Look: Living Through
Psychoanalysis and Culture in Japan*. Tokyo: Iwasaki Gakujutsu
Shuppansha Co. Ltd, 2010.

7 See Michael Balint (1952), *Primary Love and Psycho-Analytic
Technique*. London: Tavistock, 1965.

8 Takeo Doi, *Anatomy of Dependence*, p. 22.

9 See *The True Story of Ah Q* pp. x–xxxiv, (p. xxx).

10 Ibid., pp. xxxiii–xxxiv

11 In *Freud Along the Ganges*.

12 Ibid., p. 342.

13 Ibid., p. 343.

14 '... although there is comparatively little about the mother-child
relation within Freud's theory, we might say that he represented
this recognition of it in the creation of the analytic set up. The
psychoanalytic process constitutes a memory of this primary
relation, and the psychoanalyst's practice is a form of counter-
transference, since he recollects by enactment the transformational
object situation. What Freud could not analyze in himself – his
relation to his own mother – he represented through his creation of
the psychoanalytic space and process. Unless we can grasp that as
psychoanalysts we are enacting this early paradigm, we continue
to act out Freud's blindness in the countertransference.' From
Bollas, 'The transformational object' in *The Shadow of the Object*,
pp. 13–29, (p. 26).

15 The same can be said of almost all the movements of psychoanalysis: Kleinian, Lacanian, Bionian, Kohutian, Relational.
However valuable each school of thought is, all are extremist and
by eliminating the other perspectives (each of which attends to
part of the overall truth) proceed blinded by the power of negative
hallucination. I have discussed this issue in 'What is theory' in *The
Freudian Moment*, pp. 71–83.

16 See 'Vicissitudes of being, knowing, and experiencing in the therapeutic situation' in Kahn, *The Privacy of the Self*, pp. 203–18, (p.
204)

17 See 'Metapsychological and clinical aspects of regression within the psycho-analytical set-up' (1954) in *Through Paediatrics to Psycho-Analysis*, pp. 278–94, (p. 284).

18 By and large, contemporary Lacanian practitioners (outside of Paris) have abandoned the core of Lacan's technique and are Lacanian in name only. So, for example, they have marginalized the function of punctuation and provide quite lucid and lengthy interpretations to their analysands.

19 See Maurice Blanchot, 'The essential solitude' (1955) in *The Space of Literature*.

20 Ibid., pp. 26–7.

Chapter Thirteen

1 See *The Poems of Mao Zedong*, pp. 65–6.

2 For an account of Mao's intellectual history please see Willis Barnstone's 'Introduction' to *The Poems of Mao Zedong*.

Bibliography

Addiss, Stephen and Lombardo, Stanley (trans.), *Tao Te Ching*. Indianapolis and Cambridge: Hackett Publishing Company, 1993.

Akhtar, Salman (ed.), *Freud Along the Ganges: Psychoanalytic Reflections on the People and Culture of India*. New York: The Other Press, 2005.

Allport, Gordon W., *Becoming*. New Haven: Yale University Press, 1955.

Austin, John L., *How To Do Things With Words*. Oxford: Oxford University Press, 1975.

Balint, Michae, (1952) *Primary Love and Psycho-Analytic Technique*. London: Tavistock, 1965.

—*The Basic Fault: Therapeutic Aspects of Regression*. London: Tavistock, 1968.

Barnstone, Willis, 'Introduction' in *The Poems of Mao Zedong*. Berkeley, CA and London: University of California Press, 1997.

Bion, Wilfred, (1961) *Experiences in Groups*. London: Tavistock, 1974.

—(1962) *Learning from Experience*. London: Karnac, 1991.

—(1963) *Elements of Psychoanalysis*. London: Karnac, 1989.

Bohm, David, (1980) *Wholeness and the Implicate Order*. London and New York: Ark, 1988.

The Book of Songs. (*Shi Jing*), trans. Arthur Waley, Joseph Allen (ed.). New York: Grove Press, 1996.

The Book of Rites (*Li Chi*). Edited by James Legge in 1885. New York: Kessinger Publishing, undated.

The Book of Changes (*I Ching*), ed. and trans. Hua-Ching Ni. Los Angeles: Seven Star Communications Group, 2007.

Bollas, Christopher, *The Shadow of the Object: Psychoanalysis of the Unthought Known*. London: Free Association Books, 1987.

—'Le langage secret de la mère et de l'enfant' in *Nouvelle Revue de Psychanalyse*, Automne 1976. Paris: Gallimard, 1976.

—*Forces of Destiny: Psychoanalysis and Human Idiom*. London: Free Association Books, 1989.

—'Masud Khan – portrait of an extraordinary psychoanalytic personality' in *The Guardian*, June 26 1989, p. 39.

—*Being A Character: Psychoanalysis and Self Experience*. New York: Hill & Wang, 1992. London: Routledge, 1993.

—*Cracking Up: The Work of Unconscious Experience*. London: Routledge, 1995.

—*The Mystery of Things*, London: Routledge, 1999.

—*The Freudian Moment*. London: Karnac Books, 2007.

—*The Evocative Object World*. London: Routledge, 2009.

—*The Infinite Question*. London: Routledge, 2009.

Blanchot, Maurice, (1955) *The Space of Literature*, trans. Ann Smock. Lincoln: University of Nebraska Press, 1989.

Bobrow, Joseph, *Zen And Psychotherapy: Partners in Liberation*. New York: W. W. Norton, 2010.

Bohm, David, (1980) *Wholeness and the Implicate Order*. London and New York: Ark, 1988.

Bownas, Geoffrey and Thwaite, Anthony, *The Penguin Book of Japanese Verse*. London: Penguin Classics, 2009.

Buswell, Robert E., Jr., *Cultivating Original Enlightment: Wŏnhyo's Exposition of the Vajrasamadhi-Sutra*. Honolulu: University of Hawaii Press, 2007.

Chinul, (1158–1210) *Tracing Back the Radiance: Chinul's Korean Way of Zen,* Robert E. Buswell, Jr. (ed.). Honolulu, University of Hawaii, 1983; Kuroda edition,1991.

Chuang Tzu, *Chuang Tzu: Basic Writings,* trans. Burton Watson. New York: Columbia University Press, 1996.

Confucius, *Analects*, trans. Edward Slingerland. Indianapolis and Cambridge: Hackett Publishing Company, 2003.

Cornell, William F., *Explorations in Transactional Analysis: The Meech Lake Papers*. International Transactional Analysis Association, 2008.

Doi, Takeo *The Anatomy of Dependence: The Key Analysis of Japanese Behavior*, trans. John Bester (2nd edn). Tokyo: Kodansha International, 1981.

Epstein, Mark, *Thoughts Without A Thinker.* New York: Basic Books, 1995.

Freud, Sigmund, (1900) 'The Interpretation of Dreams' in *The Standard Edition of The Complete Psychological Works of Sigmund Freud*. Vol. IV. London: Hogarth Press, 1995.

—(1909) 'Notes upon a case of obsessional neurosis' in *Standard Edition*, Vol. X, pp. 153–320.

—(1915) 'The Unconscious' in *Standard Edition* Vol. XIV, pp. 161–215.

—(1921) 'Group psychology and the analysis of the ego' in *Standard Edition*, Vol. XVIII, pp. 67–143.

Fulton, Bruce and Kwon, Youngmin, (eds), *Modern Korean Fiction*. New York: Columbia, 2005.

Gernet, Jacques, *A History of Chinese Civilization*. Cambridge: Cambridge University Press, 2008.

Gu, Ming Dong (2006) 'The filial piety complex: variations on the Oedipus theme in Chinese literature and culture' in *The Psychoanalytic Quarterly*. 75: 163–95.

—*Chinese Theories of Reading and Writing: A Route to Hermeneutics and Open Poetics.* Albany: State University of New York Press, 2005.

—*Chinese Theories of Fiction: A Non-Western Narrative System.* Albany: State University of New York Press, 2006.

Hall, David L. and Ames, Roger T., *Anticipating China: Thinking Through The Narratives of Chinese and Western Culture*. Albany: State University of New York Press, 1995.

—*Dao De Jing: 'Making This Life Significant'*. New York: Random House, 2003.

Hartmann, Heinz, (1939) *Ego Psychology and the Problem of Adaptation*, trans. David Rapaport. New York: International Universities Press, 1958.

Hass, Robert, *Praise*. New York: The Ecco Press 1974.

—(ed.), *The Essential Haiku: Versions of Basho, Buson and Issa.* New York: Ecco, 1994.

Hinton, David (ed.), *Classical Chinese Poetry: An Anthology*. New York: Farrar, Strous and Giroux, 2008.

Hsün Tzu. *Hsün Tzu: Basic Writings*, trans. Burton Watson. New York: Columbia University Press, 1996.

Jennings, Pilar, *Mixing Minds: The Power of Relationships in Psychoanalysis and Buddhism.* Boston: Wisdom Publications, 2010.

Jung, C. G., 'Psychology and Religion: West and East' in Vol. 11 of the *Collected Works of C.G. Jung*. Princeton: Princeton University Press, 1989, pp. 589–608.

—*The Basic Writings of C.G. Jung*, Violet S. de Laszlo (ed.), trans. R. F. C. Hull. Princeton: Princeton University Press, 1990.

Khan, Masud, *The Privacy of the Self*. London: Hogarth Press, 1973.

—'Silence as Communication' (1963) in *The Privacy of the Self*, pp. 168–80.

—'Vicissitudes of Being, Knowing and Experiencing in the Therapeutic Situation' in (1969) *The Privacy of the Self*, pp. 203–18.

—'Regression and Integration in the Analytic Setting' (1960) in *The Privacy of the Self*, pp. 136–67.

—'The Finding and Becoming of Self' in *The Privacy of the Self*, pp. 294–305.

Kitaro, Nishida (1941) *Intuition and Reflection in Self-Consciousness*. Albany: State University of New York, 1987.

Kitayama, Osamu. *Prohibition of Don't Look: Living through Psychoanalysis and Culture in Japan*. Tokyo: Iwasaki Gakujutsu Shuppansha Co. Ltd, 2010.

Lacan, Jacques, (1973) *The Four Fundamental Concepts of Psycho-Analysis*. London: Hogarth Press, 1977.

—(1970) *Ecrits*. New York and London: W. W. Norton, 2006.

Lao Tzu, *Tao Te Ching & Hua Hu Ching*, trans. Hua-Ching Ni. Los Angeles: Seven Star Communications, 2008.

—*Dao De Jing: Making This Life Significant*, ed. and trans. Roger T. Ames and David L. Hall. New York: Ballantine, 2003.

—*Tao Te Ching*, trans. by Stephen Addiss and Stanley Lombardo. Indianapolis/Cambridge: Hackett Publishing Company, 1993.

Lawrence, Gordon (ed.), *Social Dreaming and Work*. London: Karnac, 1998.

Lee, Peter H., *Modern Korean Literature*. Honolulu: University of Hawaii Press, 1990.

Lee, Peter H., *The Columbia Anthology of Traditional Korean Poetry*. New York: Columbia University Press, 2002.

Lee, Peter H., and de Bary, Wm. Theodore, *Sources of Korean Tradition: Volume One: From Early Times Through the Sixteenth Century*. New York: Columbia, 1997.

Lee, Peter H., Yongho Ch'oe and de Bary, Wm. Theodore (eds), *Sources of Korean Tradition: Volume Two From the Sixteenth to the Twentieth Centuries*. New York: Columbia, 2000.

Lee Seung-Hwan, et al., *Anthology of Korean Studies, Volume VI*. Seoul and Elizabeth, NJ: Hollym International Corporation, 2004.

Lindquist, Cecilia, *China: Empire of Living Symbols*. Cambridge, MA: Da Capo Press, 2008.

Li Po, *The Selected Poems of Li Po* trans. David Hinton. London: Anvil Press Poetry, 2010.

Littleton, C. Scott (ed.), *The Sacred East: Hinduism, Buddhism, Confucianism, Daoism, Shinto*. London: Macmillan, 1996.

Lu Xun, *The Story of Ah Q*, trans. Yang Xianyi and Gladys Yang. Hong Kong: The Chinese University Press, 2003.

Mao Tse Tung, *Quotations From Chairman Mao Tse-Tsung*, Lin Piao (ed.). People's Republic of China, 1966.

Mao Zedong, *The Poems of Mao Zedong*. Berkeley, CA and London: The University of California Press, 1997.

—*On the Correct Handling of Contradictions Among the People*, Peking: Foreign Language Press, 1957

Mason, R. H. P and Caiger, J. G., *A History of Japan*. Tokyo: Tuttle, 1997.

McCann, David (ed.), *The Columbia Anthology of Modern Korean Poetry*. New York: Columbia University Press, 2004.

McDougall, Bonnie S. and Kam, Louie, *The Literature of China in the Twentieth Century*. New York: Columbia University Press, 1997.

Mencius (4th century BCE) *Mencius*, trans. D. C. Lau. London: Penguin, 2003.

Mente, Boye Lafayette De, *The Chinese Mind: Understanding Traditional Chinese Beliefs And Their Influence On Contemporary Culture.* Tokyo: Tuttle, 2009.

Molino, Anthony (ed.), *The Couch and the Tree: Dialogues in Psychoanalysis and Buddhism*. New York: North Point Press, 1998.

Mo Tzu (5th century BCE), *Mo Tzu: Basic Writings*, trans. Burton Watson. New York and London: Columbia, 1963.

Murasaki Shikibu, *The Tale of Genji*. New York: Penguin, 2003.

Nishitani Keiji, *Nishida Kitaro.* Berkeley, CA and London: University of California Press, 1991.

Ong, Walter, *Interfaces of the Word*. New York and London: Cornell University Press, 1977.

Piontelli, Alessandra, *From Fetus to Child: An Observational and Psychoanalytic Study*. London and New York: Routledge, 1992.

Po Chu-I, *The Selected Poems of Po Chu-I*, trans. David Hinton. New York: New Directions Books, 1999.

Pu Songling, *Strange Tales from a Chinese Studio*. London: Penguin, 2006.

Roheim, Geza, (1950) *Psychoanalysis and Anthropology.* New York: International Universities Press, 1969.

Rosenfeld, Herbert A., (1965) *Psychotic States: A Psycho-Analytical Approach*. London: Maresfield Reprints,1982.

—*Impasse and Interpretation.* London: Tavistock, 1987.

Rotem, Oman (ed.), 'Buddhism' in *The Sacred East*. Littleton. London: Macmillan, 1996.

Rubin, Jeffrey B., 'Psychoanalytic and Buddhist history and theory' in *Freud Along the Ganges: Psychoanalytic Reflections on the People and Culture of India*, Salman Akhtar (ed.), pp. 335–58.

—*Psychotherapy and Buddhism.* New York: Plenum Press, 1996.

Slingerland, Edward, 'Introduction' in *Confucius: Analects*. Indianapolis and Cambridge: Hackett Publishing Company, 2003, pp. xiii–xxv.

Suzuki, Takao, *Words in Context*: *A Japanese Perspective on Language and Culture*. Tokyo: Kodansha International Ltd, 2001.

Tu Fu, *The Selected Poems of Tu Fu*, trans. David Hinton. London: Anvil Press, 1990.

Vaidyanathan T. G. and Jeffrey, Kripal J., (eds) *Vishnu on Freud's Desk*. Oxford: Oxford University Press, 1999.

Vernant, Jean-Pierre, (1974) *Myth and Society in Ancient Greece*. New York: Zone Books, 1988.

Wang Wei, *The Selected Poems of Wang Wei*, trans. David Hinton. London: Anvil Press Poetry, 2009.

Watt, Ian, *The Rise of the Novel*. Berkeley CA and London: University of California Press, 1965.

Wilhelm, Hellmut and Wilhelm, Richard. *Understanding the I Ching*. Princeton: Princeton University Press, 1995.

Winnicott, D. W., (1965) *The Maturational Process and the Facilitating Environment*. London: Hogarth Press, 1972.

—'The Theory of the parent-infant relationship' (1960) in *The Maturational Process and the Facilitating Environment,* pp. 37–55.

—'Ego Integration in Child Development' (1962) in *The Maturational Process and the Facilitating Environment*, pp. 56–63.

—'Ego Distortion in Terms of True and False Self' (1960) in *The Maturational Process and the Facilitating Environment*, pp. 140–52.

—'The Aims of Psycho-Analytical Treatment' (1962) in *The Maturational Processes and the Facilitating Environment*, pp. 166–70.

—(1958) *Through Paediatrics to Psycho-Analysis.* London: Hogarth Press, 1975.

—'Anxiety Associated with Insecurity' (1952) in *Through Paediatrics to Psycho-Analysis*, pp. 97–100.

—'Metapsychological and Clinical Aspects of Regression within the Psycho-Analytical Set-Up' in *Through Paediatrics to Psycho-Analysis,* pp. 278–94.

—(1968) 'The concept of a healthy individual' in *Home is Where We Start From*. London: Penguin, 1968.

—(1971) *Playing and Reality*. London: Penguin 1974 and London: Routledge, 2005.

—'Dreaming, fantasying and living' in *Playing and Reality* (2005), pp. 35–50.

—*Human Nature*. London: Free Association Books, 1988.

Wŏnhyo (617–686) *Cultivating Original Enlightenment: Wŏnhyo's Exposition of the Vajrasamadhi-Sutra*, trans. Robert E. Buswell, Jr. in *Collected Works of Wŏnhyo*, Vol 1. Honolulu, University of Hawaii Press, 2007.

Yeh, Michelle (ed.), *Anthology of Modern Chinese Poetry*. New Haven and London: Yale University Press 1992.

Yip, Wai-Lim, *Chinese Poetry: An Anthology of Major Modes And Genres*. Durham, NC and London: Duke University Press, 1997.

Zhuangzi, *Basic Writings,* trans. Burton Watson. New York: Columbia University Press, 2003.

Index